NEW DIRECTIONS FOR COMMUNITY COLLEGES

Arthur M. Cohen
EDITOR-IN-CHIEF

Florence B. Brawer
ASSOCIATE EDITOR

Models for Conducting Institutional Research

Peter R. MacDougall
Santa Barbara City College

Jack Friedlander
Santa Barbara City College

EDITORS

Number 72, Winter 1990

JOSSEY-BASS INC., PUBLISHERS
San Francisco

EDUCATIONAL RESOURCES INFORMATION CENTER

ERIC Clearinghouse For Junior Colleges

UNIVERSITY OF CALIFORNIA, LOS ANGELES

MODELS FOR CONDUCTING INSTITUTIONAL RESEARCH
Peter R. MacDougall, Jack Friedlander (eds.)
New Directions for Community Colleges, no. 72
Volume XVIII, number 4
Arthur M. Cohen, Editor-in-Chief
Florence B. Brawer, Associate Editor

Microfilm copies of issues and articles are available in 16mm and 35mm, as well as microfiche in 105mm, through University Microfilms Inc., 300 North Zeeb Road, Ann Arbor, Michigan 48106.

LC 85-644753   ISSN 0194-3081   ISBN 1-55542-804-5

NEW DIRECTIONS FOR COMMUNITY COLLEGES is part of The Jossey-Bass Higher and Adult Education Series and is published quarterly by Jossey-Bass Inc., Publishers (publication number USPS 121-710) in association with the ERIC Clearinghouse for Junior Colleges. Second-class postage paid at San Francisco, California, and at additional mailing offices. Postmaster: Send address changes to Jossey-Bass Inc., Publishers, 350 Sansome Street, San Francisco, California 94104.

THE MATERIAL in this publication is based on work sponsored wholly or in part by the Office of Educational Research and Improvement, U.S. Department of Education, under contract number RI-88-062002. Its contents do not necessarily reflect the views of the Department, or any other agency of the U.S. Government.

EDITORIAL CORRESPONDENCE should be sent to the Editor-in-Chief, Arthur M. Cohen, at the ERIC Clearinghouse for Junior Colleges, University of California, Los Angeles, California 90024.

Cover photograph by Rene Sheret, Los Angeles, California © 1990.

Printed on acid-free paper in the United States of America.

EDITORS' NOTES

From state legislatures, state governing boards, accrediting commissions, and community college leaders, the call has gone out for greater understanding of how effective community colleges are in achieving desired results. Recent mandates from state and accrediting agencies are requiring colleges to provide evidence of their success in such areas as basic skills and remediation, general education, major-field content, student development, transfer effectiveness, job training, job placement, and fiscal accountability. This emphasis on measuring students' learning and performance is a significant departure from external agencies' past practices, which have focused on such things as faculty credentials, number of books in the library, teacher-to-student ratios, quality of facilities, and cost per full-time student.

The scope of the questions that institutions are now being asked to address requires colleges to gather data on their effectiveness and to use this information for improvement of programs. Therefore, institutional research can no longer be regarded as a nonessential function or as a function that merely meets compliance criteria. To effectively meet state mandates for accountability and to improve instructional programs, the institutional research function will have to be integrated into the fundamental processes of the college's operation.

Basic to the institution's ability to respond effectively to calls for measures of institutional effectiveness is its ability to establish systematic procedures for identifying, gathering, analyzing, and reporting necessary information. Community colleges vary significantly in size, complexity, resources, research expertise, and commitment to institutional research. This volume, in addition to describing some contemporary mandates for institutional effectiveness, presents a range of institutional research models that can be used to seek answers to the complex questions being posed. We have purposely sought a broad sampling of organizational approaches to institutional research, with the expectation that this range of options will be valuable to the institution determining its approach to institutional research.

To help the reader develop a clear understanding of the research models, and to allow for comparisons, the authors of each chapter were asked to describe their models by answering seven questions:

1. *How are the research objectives determined?*
   a. Who is involved in determining the research objectives? How and why are these people selected?
   b. Who ultimately decides the research agenda?
2. *How are the procedures and responsibilities for carrying out the research program established?*

    a. Who provides operational leadership for implementing the research agenda?

    b. Who is responsible for carrying out the research project? One person? Several staff members?

    c. What are the roles of the chief executive officer, vice-presidents, deans, and college committees?

    d. What benefits are realized through these procedures, by contrast with other procedures that could be followed?

3. *How are research projects monitored?*

    a. How is the implementation of the research program monitored, to ensure that objectives are being achieved?

    b. Who decides on adjustments to the institutional research agenda?

4. *What is the process for identifying the results and implications of the research?*

    a. Who is responsible for critically analyzing the research results and for determining the adequacy of the methods followed and the soundness of the conclusions drawn?

    b. Who is responsible for determining the research's implications for changing institutional practices?

5. *Who determines which institutional changes will be made as a result of the research?*

    a. How is the practicality of the suggested changes determined?

    b. How are the procedures for implementing changes determined? Who is responsible for implementing changes, committing resources, and establishing schedules?

    c. How are the short-term and long-term benefits of the institutional research program evaluated (cost-benefit analysis)?

6. *How are the results of the research studies disseminated?* To whom are the research results disseminated, and how?

7. *What are the strengths and weaknesses of this research model?* Outline the strengths and weaknesses of your model.

Each author was also asked to describe how a research study was conducted within the model's framework (the related section of each chapter is intended to demonstrate how the model is applied in carrying out the research function).

    In Chapter One, Julie Slark examines the traditional approach to community college research by presenting an overview of the centralized research model at Rancho Santiago College, in California. Slark demonstrates that, although research is coordinated in a single office, the goal of developing broad-based staff involvement in research can be enhanced through flexible staffing of the research office and integration of the research function into the governance components of the college.

    John Losak, in Chapter Two, describes the centralized research model of a multicampus district. In this model, the research function is operated by staff in the district's central office, who assume responsibility for conducting all phases of the institutional research program.

In Chapter Three, Janis Cox Jones describes a district-coordinated institutional research model in a multicampus community college district. This model uses a centralized office of institutional research at the district headquarters, as well as research coordinators at each of the three colleges in the district. Jones describes how the district- and campus-based research efforts are coordinated and integrated into the governance processes of the district and the individual colleges.

A decentralized research model is explained in Chapter Four. In this approach, the institutional research program is conducted by a committee, rather than by a manager. The committee is composed of staff members drawn from various areas of the college. Peter R. MacDougall, Jack Friedlander, Elaine Cohen, and John Romo describe the decentralized model, as well as its relationship to the objectives of connecting research results with institutional change and establishing research as a value in the college's culture.

Chapter Five presents a hybrid of the models featured in Chapters One and Four. Marylin Orton describes the centralized-decentralized approach at Allan Hancock College, in California. This model involves a 60-percent-time institutional researcher, whose activities are guided by an institutional research committee.

A number of community colleges have voluntarily entered regional, state, and national consortia for conducting institutional research. In Chapter Six, Don Doucette and Jeffrey A. Seybert describe the model used by a Kansas consortium of community colleges formed to meet research-based accountability goals. In describing the consortium's structure and operations, Doucette and Seybert offer valuable insights into the advantages and limitations of a consortium, insights that should be helpful to those considering consortia for institutional research.

In Chapter Seven, Daniel D. McConochie and James D. Tschechtelin describe the state agency–community college cooperative model, used in Maryland, for conducting institutional research. Staff from the Maryland State Board for Community Colleges work cooperatively with a voluntary statewide research organization composed of individuals responsible for institutional research at each of the state's seventeen community colleges. McConochie and Tschechtelin note that the state agency's collaboration with local colleges enables the research needs of the state board and of the individual colleges to be met with minimal duplication of effort and makes projects possible that could not be initiated with the data and resources of a single institution.

In New Jersey, colleges are expected to document their accomplishments in a number of areas, including basic skills and remediation, general education, achievements in the major field, students' satisfaction, and students' personal development. In Chapter Eight, Madan Capoor and Edward Morante describe two state-mandated programs for institutional accountability and the working relationship between a state agency and the state colleges. The model used in New Jersey provides a means by which state-mandated institutional research can be accomplished through collaboration between a state's higher education agency and the state's colleges and universities.

In Chapter Nine, Jack Friedlander and Peter R. MacDougall review the recent growth in the institutional assessment movement and examine community colleges' responses to state mandates for measuring students' performance. They offer recommendations for community colleges to meet state requirements while simultaneously improving teaching and learning. Community college leaders are urged to become actively involved in shaping statewide approaches to accountability that will benefit the state, the institutions, teachers, and students.

Peter R. MacDougall
Jack Friedlander
Editors

Peter R. MacDougall is president of Santa Barbara City College.

Jack Friedlander is dean of academic affairs at Santa Barbara City College.

The centralized research model has the advantage of closely coordinating an institution's research activities.

The Traditional Centralized Model of Institutional Research

Julie Slark

Rancho Santiago College's institutional research program enjoys the reputation among California community colleges of being a stable, long-enduring, highly visible, traditional, centralized college function. The program has matured over the years and developed into an effective, integral part of the college's decision-making process. This accomplishment is due primarily to the program's use of the traditional centralized research model, augmented by alternative approaches.

Rancho Santiago College (RSC) serves 21,000 students in for-credit courses and another 15,000 students in continuing education on two campuses, at three major sites, and at many other community locations. The student body is very diverse in terms of age, ethnicity, and educational objectives, and programs are very comprehensive, to meet diverse needs. The college employs approximately 200 full-time faculty, serves a community population of 450,000, and is in an urban-suburban center of Orange County, adjacent to the Los Angeles County metropolis. The institutional research program was established in 1974.

Organizational Structure

The success of this institutional research model reflects the organizational structure in which it exists and the leadership style of the top administrators. The director of research and planning reports to the chancellor, who is an advocate of institutional research, not only as an administrative support but also as an integral support to all levels and departments of the institution. One reason why the director reports to the chancellor is the belief that this arrangement encourages more objectivity in research than would be likely if the research program were in a separate division or unit. Furthermore, this organizational structure reinforces the concept of institutional research as a function in support of the entire institution, rather than as one solely in support of educational programs or administrative activities.

This model assumes a broad base of responsibility for institutional research. It also rests on the concept of the research function's integration into the day-to-day operations of the college, an arrangement brought about through the close working relationship between the director of research and planning and the chancellor's cabinet. The cabinet consists of the three vice-chancellors, the director of personnel, and the executive assistant to the chancellor. The director of research and planning participates frequently in the weekly cabinet meetings and in other functions involving cabinet members. Many research-related decisions are made in that forum. Regular interaction between the cabinet and the director of research and planning keeps everyone informed of research-related institutional needs and research findings and of activities that may be helpful to individual programs. As a member of the chancellor's staff, the director of research and planning is also responsible for coordinating college planning. The importance of the relationship between the planning and research functions is recognized in that both are coordinated in one office. The planning-implementation-evaluation cycle is enhanced by this structure.

Before the model being presented here can be described fully, the governance structure of the college must be described. Six councils—on external affairs, planning, finance, curriculum, student services, and human resources—include among their members appointees of the faculty academic senate, the classified (noninstructional) staff liaison group, and the management staff liaison groups. Each council refers recommendations to a specified vice-chancellor (or to the chancellor, in the case of the planning council). The research committee is a subcommittee of the college planning council.

The research committee and the planning council provide additional mechanisms for interaction between the centralized research program and the representatives of departments and employee constituencies. In this way, the use of research findings is facilitated by the audience and participation available in the planning council and the research committee. Moreover, research becomes a more relevant topic because the director of research and planning remains informed and participates in frequent, structured interactions with faculty and staff about important issues.

Relationships with Other Departments. Relationships between the institutional research office and other departments are formalized through the structures just described, and research activities become credible because they reflect the institutional priorities established by the councils, the chancellor, and the cabinet. For example, while the data-processing and institutional research departments are not organizationally related, institutional researchers are assured of data processing's full cooperation because their requests for support reflect the needs identified by the decision-making bodies of the college, and so there are seldom any problems in departmental relationships or in access to data-processing services.

Good working relationships between institutional research and all other departments are crucial to the success of a research program. Institutional researchers often struggle to overcome others' perceptions that research is threatening and intimidating. Management techniques, which may include the use of institutional research, are not always consistent with academicians' notions of collegial governance. It is the responsibility of researchers to create consistent mechanisms for "mainstreaming" the institutional research function. At RSC, interdepartmental relationships are facilitated by the organizational structure and informal relationships developed through campus activities.

Researchers as Campus and Team Leaders. The director of research and planning is an institutional leader and active member of the college team, rather than an isolated actor. Some kinds of research, such as assessment of institutional effectiveness or classroom-based research, require the leadership of an individual or a group before they can begin. At RSC, the director of research and planning introduces such topics to the appropriate groups (usually the planning council, the research committee, and the cabinet) or individual departments.

Other Decentralized College Research Activities. While the RSC model is a centralized one, it is enhanced by many decentralized components, which are increasing in number as research awareness increases. For example, many faculty members and departments have taken it upon themselves to engage in research, such as student follow-up studies, needs assessment for programs, assessment of students' learning, and evaluation of programs' effectiveness. The institutional research office provides assistance, if requested to do so. If these types of activities continue to increase, they should further the conditions that encourage integration of the research function.

Implementing the Model

Creating the Research Agenda. Every year, a research agenda is developed for specific priorities and studies to be implemented. At the end of each academic year, the director of research and planning reviews the status of the current year's projects, to determine which ones need to be continued or augmented. The director also assesses the need for research in new areas and meets with the chancellor's cabinet for suggestions. A proposed agenda is then developed and submitted to the research committee, where it may be modified before being forwarded (in the form of recommendations) to the planning council. The chancellor discusses the recommended agenda with the cabinet and reports decisions to the planning council and the director of research and planning.

This agenda provides the institutional research office's work plan for the following academic year. It is referred to frequently in decisions on day-to-day priorities and in responses to requests for additional research, which are made throughout the year. The agenda and the process through which it is developed are helpful politically in requesting assistance from other departments, responding to questions about the purpose or intent of a study, disseminating research findings, and using the findings in decision making. The agenda always includes regular or annual studies; for example, research is conducted each year on transfer students, demographics, enrollment trends, students' characteristics, retention, and learning outcomes. Research needs that have not been included in the agenda may be presented throughout the year by various sources (one of the councils, the cabinet, a faculty or staff member, an external agency, or the director of research and planning). More often than not, the director is able to accommodate new requests. If not, the director confers with the chancellor, the research committee, or the cabinet for assistance in setting priorities. The Rancho Santiago Community College District board of trustees is kept informed of the new research agenda and of the progress toward its fulfillment. The board also is kept informed of research studies, through oral and written reports presented during the year.

Who Conducts the Research? The regular, full-time, college-funded institutional research staff consists of the director, an administrative secretary, and up to twelve additional part-time or grant-funded employees in various positions. The current staff in the Office of Research and Planning is made up of a full-time grant-funded research analyst; a three-quarters-time grant-funded research analyst; a three-month, half-time grant-funded research analyst; a full-time faculty member with 20 percent release time for conducting research in the Office of Research and Planning; a 40 percent-time grant-funded grants assistant; an adjunct psychology faculty member, who works regularly in the office; a nineteen-hour-a-week general office clerk; three student assistants; and a high school work-experience student. An administrative intern from a doctoral program was employed full-time for one semester, and consultants are occasionally hired with grant funds for specific projects.

Diverse part-time staff have been used to provide flexibility in several areas: to match skills and staffing levels with the needs of current projects, to maximize cost efficiency, and (in the case of faculty members) to bring the teaching perspective to institutional research. The five faculty members who have participated in the release-time project for faculty research report having been enriched by the additional perspective acquired through that experience. Noninstructional professional staff from other departments have also worked on a temporary basis in the research office. The synergism produced through this multifaceted staffing arrangement has become invaluable in the effort to integrate the research program into collegewide activities. Over time, the base for institutional research will expand.

The director supervises all staff members and assigns projects according to the staff's talents and areas of interest. Staff are assigned specific projects, and regular staff meetings are held to review them. Strategies for research design and project implementation are developed by the director, in cooperation with individual staff members, who carry out the implementation phase. Before implementation, research designs are discussed with staff members in related programs and, occasionally, with the research committee or the cabinet. The director apprises the chancellor of any significant matters. Thus, the director supervises all projects, is responsible for all phases of each project, speaks for all projects, and chooses the appropriate bodies with which to coordinate efforts. In almost every research project, however, the chancellor, the cabinet, the research committee, assigned research staff, and staff in related programs are principal actors.

Reporting, Disseminating, and Using Research Findings. Reports of research findings are prepared through the same processes and with the same bodies just described. Staff of the programs involved in research studies are consulted before reports are written or after drafts have been prepared. Close contact is maintained with these staff members throughout the duration of a research project. Before reports are published, drafts are always reviewed with the program staff and the research committee and sometimes with the cabinet as well. The review phase helps report writers identify the most important findings.

Research reports do not include program recommendations, although they do state (in executive summaries or conclusions) issues that require further attention. Since program decisions are made with politics, personnel, the budget, and even intuitive concerns in mind, besides taking account of related research findings, RSC research publications do not presume to include recommendations. The research reports are clearly written enough for staff members to understand the research's implications for policymaking, which takes place at the program level and in the councils, the cabinet, and the board of trustees.

Research findings are disseminated through the research committee, the cabinet, and staff of related programs. Other means of dissemination are far-reaching and include institutional research newsletters regularly distributed to all staff, presentations to various college groups, and open-forum "brown bag" noontime sessions; there cannot be too many dissemination mechanisms. The director's membership in numerous college committees is another vehicle for communicating the research perspective. The research advocacy of top administrators is also helpful. Most important, however, is the development of an environment where the research function is integrated into the operations of the entire college. This is the most valuable means of enhancing research use.

How the Model Works

The structure described in this chapter for developing an agenda, conducting research, and disseminating findings is the standard format followed at RSC. The complete process, however (identification of research needs, designing and implementation of studies, analysis, review, publication, dissemination and use of findings) has differed slightly for each study conducted, since the college organization is healthy and fluid. As such, it uses the standard format as the ideal but remains flexible enough to accommodate changing variables.

The following example illustrates how the standard format works. Before the creation of the research committee, one research staff member interacted frequently with RSC counselors and deans in the academic division, to help them develop new policies and procedures for student assessment and course placement. Through these interactions, this staff member determined that there was a need for research to examine the relationship between basic-skills test scores and students' success in the specific courses in which they had been placed, so that the new policies and procedures would be effective, equitable, and justifiable. After consulting with the director of research and planning, this staff member (a faculty member working in the research office) conducted the study, which was designed in consultation with interested academic deans. Before publishing the possibly controversial results, he reviewed the findings with the deans, who offered narrative suggestions. The findings were widely disseminated and provided the cover story for a research newsletter. Along with other concerns and issues, they have been significant contributors to RSC's current policies on course placement and prerequisites. Debate surrounding this topic has gone on for months, however, as have references to that study, and even after the creation of the research committee the debate has continued. The director of research and planning had kept the committee members apprised of similar research in other community colleges, and members of the committee recently requested further research on predictors of academic success, because time has passed and conditions have changed since the first study. As a result, this topic was placed on the proposed research agenda, and the study was assigned to the same staff member who conducted the first one.

Advantages and Disadvantages of the Centralized Model

The centralized approach to research has the obvious advantage of closely coordinating an institution's research activities. This practice avoids duplication of effort, reveals gaps in the institution's research knowledge, and allows a focus on the changes that will result from the research. A centralized office that includes at least one person solely responsible for institutional research can devote undivided attention to the research program. With the centralized model, faculty, staff, board members, and even the community know where to turn when a research-related need arises. Institutional research becomes a credible, sanctioned college function. A centralized office is most easily (and most frequently) staffed by professionals trained in conducting research. Study findings may be more objective and certainly are more credible when they are developed by an independent office. With research centralized, it is also easier to coordinate it with planning.

The major disadvantage of this model is that the research function is separate, and so the researcher may not be familiar enough with the full range of perspectives and with the subtleties of educational programs and services. Furthermore, because the function is separate, the researcher is sometimes seen as an outsider, and perceptions of the threatening nature of research and evaluation are heightened. Researchers need to remain connected with programs and services, faculty and staff, decision making, and operational activities, in order to enhance the contributions of institutional research.

At RSC, the advantages of the centralized approach are seen as significant. As this chapter has described, we employ extensive strategies to ensure that the research function is connected with the day-to-day operation of programs.

Julie Slark is director of research, planning, and special projects for the Rancho Santiago Community College District, Santa Ana, California.

*This chapter examines a centralized research model in a
multicampus district and the model's role in policy formation
and decision making.*

The Centralized Research Model in
a Multicampus District

John Losak

How a multicampus institution addresses the various political, economic,
and efficiency issues surrounding the decision for centralization versus
decentralization of its various administrative offices is an ongoing, dynamic
process. Resolved differently among institutions and even within the same
institution from one occasion to the next, the choice for centralization or
decentralization necessarily influences the functions and operations of
particular administrative areas, such as institutional research.

In many community colleges, institutional research is likely to be
restricted to the role of completing state and federal reports and developing
enrollment projections. In a few community colleges, however, a comprehensive staff provides information to support policy formulation, planning,
and decision making. The Office of Institutional Research at Miami–Dade
Community College is an example of the latter arrangement. As a four-
campus community college, which annually enrolls 73,000 credit students
and 30,000 noncredit students and has over 840 full-time faculty, Miami–
Dade supports a centralized institutional research operation at the district level.

The scope of responsibilities assigned to institutional research at
Miami–Dade goes beyond routine support and enrollment projections, to
encompass the initiation of educational research for policy decisions and
collegewide coordination of entry-level and exit assessment of students.
This chapter examines Miami–Dade's centralized model for conducting
institutional research, by analyzing the comprehensive nature of its responsibilities and its role in the educational and administrative framework of
the college.

13

The Centralized Multicampus Model

The development of a centralized institutional research office at Miami–Dade Community College occurred over a five-year period and was undoubtedly influenced by many factors and issues, both internal and external to the institution. For many years, institutional research activities had been divided between a central office for reporting data collection and campus-based offices for testing and research. The emphasis in the campus offices was primarily on testing, with a minimum level of research activity.

Growing concern with accountability at the local and state levels was a primary force in the evolution toward centralization. This emphasis on accountability was evidenced by new state requirements for placement and follow-up of graduates, the adoption of entry-level assessment requirements (initially a policy of the institution but eventually a response to state mandates), and the emergence of exit-level testing for students who were completing lower-division programs at community colleges and universities. In addition to the state mandates for accountability, Miami–Dade implemented a number of programs to improve students' performance. It reformed its general education curriculum, computerized student advisement, certificated graduation, and tracked satisfactory academic progress. These forces—combined with the college president's interest in having access to standardized information for each campus, avoiding duplication of effort, and securing the maximum benefit from existing resources—led, in 1984, to the centralization of all research positions.

The office is led by a dean of institutional research and employs six professionals, two paraprofessionals, two secretaries, and two computer programmers. Each staff member is assigned specific areas of responsibility. For example, reports related to entry-level and exit-level assessment are handled by one individual; placement and follow-up activities are performed by another. The associate director coordinates all state and federal reporting, as well as enrollment projections. Two senior research associates are assigned as liaisons between the institutional research office and two campuses, so that each campus has an accessible contact for data requests.

To provide coordination of policies and procedures among the campuses of Miami–Dade, and to encourage faculty participation in decision making, the college president has established collegewide committees for each major function of college operations. For the institutional research function, as currently defined, a committee for research and testing is chaired by the dean of institutional research. Specific responsibilities of this committee include the following:

- Conducting research jointly as a task force, and presenting recommendations when specifically requested to do so by the president, the president's council, or the executive committee

- Analyzing the impact of changing state and federal data-reporting requirements
- Serving as a communications link between researchers from different areas of the college and facilitating familiarity with current developments, both within and outside the institution, that may be of interest to or may affect particular areas of research
- Ensuring that research projects undertaken at the campus level involve research models that can be replicated where (replication is) feasible at all campuses
- Providing continual review of the college's assessment program
- Generating an annual document on criteria for course placement.

Responsibility for collegewide coordination of both entry-level placement testing and exit-level testing, through the College-Level Academic Skills Test (CLAST), rests with the dean of institutional research. For purposes of research, this form of management is clearly advantageous because it permits immediate access to test files and creates an opportunity to generate timely, useful information. Management of these testing programs proceeds in accordance with direction provided by the research and testing committee, the academic affairs committee, and the president's council.

The research and testing committee and the academic affairs committee develop joint annual recommendations for course placement of students with low entry-level skills. Final decision-making responsibility for all assessment policies rests with the president's council. Periodic reports from the institutional research office link entry-level and exit-level test scores to curricula, monitor students' progress from year to year, and compare the results of testing with results at other institutions statewide. Advice on testing issues is provided to college administrators as they deal with these topics in local, state, and national forums.

Determining the Research Agenda

Internal Factors. Research and evaluation studies are initiated primarily to aid decision making. The determination of research topics and objectives occurs through several processes, both informally and by design, but always with flexibility. Research topics are sought from each campus via the liaison role performed by the two senior research associates. Each associate interacts regularly with assigned campus administrators, to determine which research topics most need action. Every attempt is made to keep the process simple. For example, written proposals are not required. The senior research associates are aware of resources and are thus able to accept projects, put them on hold, or reject them. Rarely are requests rejected, however, and when they are, it is almost always because their scope is too grand or data elements are unavailable.

The institutional research office is close to the district offices responsible for academic affairs, student services, and business affairs. Through daily interactions, policy issues are discussed and possible research responses are considered. The college president meets frequently with the dean of institutional research, to review the status of ongoing projects and suggest others. The collegewide research and testing committee also reviews and discusses research projects on a monthly basis. Faculty input occurs via faculty membership on the research and testing committee and through informal requests.

Miami–Dade's approach to determining research topics and objectives permits a flow of requests and ideas, through systematic interactions of institutional research staff with campus administrators, open and informal processes, and opportunities for institutional research staff to initiate projects and anticipate administrative needs. We have consistently found that if we await administrative requests, they very frequently come too close to the time when a decision is needed. Therefore, by staying current with the directions of the two-year-college movement, the requirements of state legislation, and the interests of Miami–Dade's decision makers, we can often generate information and reports well in advance of the needs perceived by administrators.

Recent areas of focus for educational research include student retention, transfer of graduates, equal access and equal opportunity, and students' progress. Research support is also provided for major collegewide projects, such as the Teaching/Learning Project and the Enrollment Management Project. These commitments were made as the projects were planned by their respective collegewide steering committees. The Teaching/Learning Project represents a comprehensive effort to improve the quality of teaching and learning, to make teaching a more professionally rewarding career, and to make teaching and learning the focal point of college activities and decision making. Each of the senior institutional research professional staff members is on a specific subcommittee of this extensive project, continually providing data and guidance for each committee.

An indeterminate amount of research is undertaken by faculty and administrators outside the central research office, primarily among those working toward doctoral degrees. Guidance and support for this activity is routinely supplied by institutional research staff. Final decisions on research projects are made by the dean of institutional research, on the basis of direction provided by the president and by the research and testing committee.

External Factors. The establishment of a centralized institutional research office, by providing a single point of contact and exchange of information, greatly enhances the opportunity for links with external agencies. Each year, the public school system supplies the college with a tape containing the names, birthdates, and class ranks of all seniors in high school. This tape is used to generate a list of seniors from each high school, which is then matched with the college's fall-term enrollment list. Class-rank data are used as a control variable when studies are conducted to compare students' performance in college as a function of their attendance at particular high schools. The college regularly reports to the public schools on the performance of their graduates as entering freshmen.

Other examples of college research projects originating from external contacts include those coordinated by the State of Florida, through the Division of Community Colleges, to establish cutoff scores for the entry-level assessment program, analyze the state university system's student data base in order to determine transfer rates and success of former Miami–Dade students, and participate in the Florida Department of Education's feedback system, which captures outcome data on graduates and dropouts. This latter project involves matching individual computerized files of enrollees and graduates against state employment files, state university system files, and Department of Defense files, in order to locate students. Any information found in the three data bases is put on computer tapes, which are returned to the individual colleges for use in state reports. The comprehensive information included in this final data base is used for feedback to occupational program managers at Miami–Dade.

Carrying Out Research

On the basis of the variety of contacts that may occur, new research projects are presented by each professional staff member at an institutional research staff conference. For reasonable projects within the purview of institutional research, there is discussion of resources, and priorities are set. Discussions are formalized through semiannual statements of research goals and objectives, generated by the professional institutional research staff. Goals include recurring assignments (for example, annual student profiles), as well as new research projects.

Internal grant funding allows the Office of Institutional Research to contract for data-collection services when issues arise that require information beyond the scope of the full-time staff. Two such issues involved the Enrollment Management Project, a research-based process for increasing enrollment and retention through a careful analysis of expectations, motivations, and limitations of the institution's enrollment program. The Enrollment Management Project called for a comprehensive survey of high school seniors, in order to determine their postgraduation plans and their perceptions of Miami–Dade and its competitors. A concurrent series of focus-group interviews was conducted with seniors, parents, and counselors in predominantly black high schools, whose graduates were not choosing to attend Miami–Dade. Both data-collection efforts were contracted out to a research corporation. Analysis of the survey results will be conducted by the Office of Institutional Research, and the focus-group study will be summarized by the outside contractor.

In most cases, a research project is carried out primarily by a professional staff member, although two persons will often coauthor a paper. The primary author, usually a staff member with a Ph.D., is responsible for a first draft of the report, which includes the usual statements of background, purpose, method, findings, and implications. Not all reports, however, are intended to be in publishable form when they are distributed within the college; the literature-review and perspective sections are often enhanced considerably before publication.

Monitoring of Research Projects

Monitoring occurs at the monthly institutional research staff meetings and the monthly research and testing committee meetings. It also occurs informally among staff members. Adjustments in priorities are suggested primarily by the college president and the dean of institutional research. The dean meets once a month with each staff member, to review his or her priority list.

Results and Implications

Campus data are available from the mainframe computer, but interpretation and perspectives are necessary for meaningful conclusions. The Office of Institutional Research interacts directly with campus vice-presidents and academic deans (and with their district counterparts, as appropriate) to secure opinions and views of the emerging report. This process deepens the involvement of administrators and tends to minimize surprises when the final report is circulated. The initial draft is reviewed by both the associate director and the dean of institutional research. It is usually returned for refinements, reviewed again, and then proofread by a staff associate.

A research report typically addresses implications for change. Nevertheless, the academic deans, student deans, campus vice-presidents, and the college president are usually more directly involved in determining such implications. The practicality of the changes suggested by research findings is deliberated by the parties who will be most affected, and any recommendations resulting from these deliberations go through the typical administrative channels. Over the past fifteen years, primarily because the current college president and his predecessor have valued the use of empirical data to inform decision making, research findings and implications have influenced decisions.

Dissemination of Results

Because effective communication of research findings remains one of the most challenging tasks of the professional in an institutional research office, Miami-Dade has adopted the approach of providing wide distribution of an abstract or executive summary. Results may be disseminated in one of several ways: a formal research report; an information capsule; memoranda; presentations at local, state, and national meetings; and publications in journals.

For each formal research report, at least 260 abstracts are distributed to key administrators and other interested parties, including members of the board of trustees. Recipients of an abstract can obtain a copy of the complete report by making a request to the institutional research office. A briefer, more informal format, the information capsule, was designed for items of information that must be made available quickly and require only a brief narrative or synopsis.

The Office of Institutional Research generates and submits statistical reports to appropriate state and federal agencies, as well as to statewide task forces and committees. These include reports on students' characteristics, credits generated, follow-up of graduates, cost analysis, performance of local public high school graduates, enrollment projects, and student profiles.

The institutional research office works with campus administrators to generate enrollment projections, and these are compared weekly with actual credits generated for various categories of students. A college factbook is also produced, to provide an overview of Miami-Dade for internal and external audiences.

Data and conceptual assistance are provided to college staff who work with the news media, prepare grant proposals, write speeches and presentations, and formulate research projects for the community as well as for the college. For example, the institutional research office was deeply involved in a recent effort to expand educational and vocational opportunities for minorities in Dade County. Institutional research staff members also serve on local, state, and national committees. They make presentations of research findings to state and national meetings, respond to data requests from outside users, and consult with visitors who want to learn more about the research function at Miami-Dade.

Strengths and Weaknesses of the Centralized Research Model

The advantages of centralizing the institutional research function include opportunities to specialize, cost efficiency, enhancement of communication with outside agencies, easier internal flow, nonduplication of effort, and more direct control by the college president. Centralization permits maximum use of the computer-programming support provided through the student, faculty, and financial master record systems stored on the mainframe. Data bases can be created, maintained, and analyzed from either a collegewide or a campus-specific perspective. Definitions, as needed, can be coordinated through the research and testing committee. Programmers have a single point of contact, standard guidelines, and more time to provide new areas of support. They can literally respond overnight to many administrative requests that require new configurations of data.

The centralized approach also permits a deliberate effort to anticipate issues, with enough lead time to generate useful data and interpret the implications. It also facilitates interaction among researchers; single individuals on each campus may well be isolated from the professional exchanges that can easily occur at a central location. The concentration of talent also permits diversification on projects. For example, consider the production of a research report. In many small offices, the professional often does everything—conceptualization, data retrieval, table building, keyboarding, and distribution. With centralization, people can specialize.

Centralization of the institutional research functions allows all areas of focus to receive more sophisticated and intensive study than would be possible if they were all being pursued by separate offices at each of the campuses. For example, comprehensive data bases have been constructed for tracking matriculation since the early 1970s, in order to evaluate various outcomes (term-by-term reenrollment, grade point averages, degrees earned); to evaluate the success of college-preparatory (remedial) classes, English as a Second Language (ESL) classes, and general education core courses; to evaluate students' performance on the CLAST; and to monitor placement of graduates according to their major fields of study.

The weaknesses of the model show up in the areas of ownership of data and control of the research function within a campus. Centralization of research at Miami–Dade has not eliminated tension deriving from legitimate concerns that the academic deans and vice-presidents raise from time to time about the lack of resources to carry out their own projects. Moreover, campus administrators lose direct control over the nature of the research to be undertaken on their students, and so there may sometimes be less interest in issues because decisions are made on a collegewide basis. Ownership of data is a major issue in virtually all research, and it takes on serious overtones when findings are unfavorable toward some aspect of an activity or function.

Application of the Model

How a centralized research function can accommodate policy demands is well illustrated by Miami–Dade's response to the State of Florida's mandate for entry-level testing. Students who score below established statewide standards must take appropriate courses in remedial mathematics, English, or reading before enrolling for college-level courses in these areas. When this policy was enacted, questions arose immediately: Should students who need remediation in all three areas be expected to take all the remedial courses during the first term? Do students who are immersed in remedial work during the initial term differ with respect to academic success from those who take only one or two remedial courses at the same time? This issue was hotly debated for some weeks at Miami-Dade, and positions were formed and strongly presented. Through intensive focus of its resources, the institutional research office addressed the question by using a retrospective cohort of students. The answer at Miami-Dade was that students not immersed in remedial courses showed better retention, earned more total credits, and had higher grade point averages. As this finding began to emerge from the data analysis, meetings were held with the research and testing committee, to encourage a critique of the report's first draft. After minor revisions, a meeting was held with the academic deans, to summarize the findings. A few individuals remained unconvinced; overall, however, the major policy implication of the findings was endorsed— that is, students would not be required to take all the needed remedial courses in the first term. In this case, the college president was confronted with data that clearly contradicted his initial recommendation. After a thorough review, he modified his position to coincide with the research findings, and a formal recommendation was made to the president's council to require that students in need of remedial courses enroll in at least one. The recommendation was formally adopted by the president's council and implemented during the next major term.

Conclusion

In educational research, student assessment, reporting, and information sharing, the centralized research model has had a visible and lasting impact. For researchers in our office, juxtaposition of these three areas, and concomitant control and access to the data bases, have fostered an unusual sensitivity to and perspective on policy issues. Combining these three areas into one centralized operation, the Office of Institutional Research has evolved into a strategically significant component of the college.

Research findings have been used externally to enhance the reputation of Miami-Dade as a leader of the community college movement. One of the overwhelming reasons why Roueche and Baker's (1987) national study ranked Miami-Dade as the top community college was the extraordinary amount of information the college collects about its students, from start to finish.

In summary, Miami-Dade's institutional research model—centralized district research in a multicampus setting—has become a uniquely valuable component of the collegewide organization, in terms of research's relationships with the internal and external environments. By consolidating these substantial areas of responsibility, the Office of Institutional Research enjoys the unusual ability to respond quickly to a broad range of information needs. The office also continues to develop data bases and methodologies for addressing the long-range educational issues that often develop beyond the confines of the institution. Clearly, as postsecondary institutions look toward student outcomes as measures of effectiveness, the particular fusion of functions that characterizes Miami–Dade's Office of Institutional Research will no doubt serve as an appropriate model for institutions that value information resources for decision making.

Reference

Roueche, J. E., and Baker, G. A., III. *Access and Excellence: The Open-Door College.* Washington, D.C.: American Association of Community and Junior Colleges, 1987. (ED 274 391)

John Losak has been at Miami–Dade Community College for twenty-five years, serving as director of counseling and testing for the first half of his tenure and as professor of psychology and education and dean of institutional research for the second half.

In a multicampus district, "coordinated decentralization" may be the best approach to fostering a focus on research and organizational change.

The Coordinated Research Model in a Multicampus District

Janis Cox Jones

The Los Rios (California) Community College District's research model has evolved over a seven-year period, from a centralized model to a district-coordinated model. A district research office and staff are responsible for the majority of research done and published by the district. Each college maintains a research office as well, to coordinate and undertake college-specific research studies. The move from centralization to district coordination resulted from growing respect for and use of research on the campuses. The change was also seen as a solution to growing concerns about competing priorities for research, quality control, and access to the district's data base.

Description of the Model

District/College Relationships. As in many other multicampus districts, a usually healthy tension exists in Los Rios between, on the one hand, the three colleges (American River College, Cosumnes River College, and Sacramento City College) and, on the other, the district office. The colleges do not wish to be perceived merely as campuses within a multicampus district; each is unique in its own right, and two of the colleges had long histories of autonomy before the district was created.

With the appointment of a chancellor who supported research and understood its usefulness as a basis of planning, decision making, and internal and external accountability, the idea of a district office for planning and research was born. In 1983, with the arrival of a director of research who had a state-policy background and of a research associate who had much experience at one of the colleges, a centralized office of planning and research was established. The research agenda was determined primarily by the director of planning and research and by the chancellor, in consultation with the college presidents.

As the district's "student flow research model" (Coffey, 1987) became recognized both statewide and nationally, and as the chancellor and the board members continued to highlight research studies and findings throughout the state, interest in and demand for research increased. Demand focused on the ability to conduct research at the college and program levels, to determine whether specific outcome initiatives were having the desired effects. While the district research office could and did handle a number of such requests, the increased emphasis on research spawned much involvement throughout the district, with a variety of faculty and administrators gathering data and issuing reports.

Types of Research. Basically, there are four different types of research conducted in the Los Rios district: districtwide, college-specific, faculty-specific, and administrator-specific research. Districtwide research is done by the district's Office of Planning and Research (OP&R), primarily for planning, evaluation, and policy purposes. The research is based on a concept of the flow of students: from the community, into and through the district's three colleges, and then beyond, as transfers to four-year institutions or as new employees into business. OP&R research analyzes programs and services from the districtwide perspective, but every study also includes data, charts, and graphs (by college), with highlights of differences among the three colleges. More recently, data have been analyzed by program as well as by college, for faculty's use in specific programs.

College-specific research includes a wide variety of reports, data analyses, and research studies. They are college-specific and designed to answer questions about the college's students and programs (such as those involving community needs assessments, program-review statistics, and curriculum-development reports) that are not covered in regular districtwide studies.

Faculty-specific studies are generally focused on classroom-based research initiatives. These studies are undertaken by faculty, either singly or cooperatively, sometimes with release time (if they are of high priority to the college) and sometimes without.

Administrator-specific studies or research requests are often for new combinations and analyses of traditional data, to answer specific policy questions about students, staffing, programs, services, or budgets. Administrators occasionally decide to take on particular research studies because of issues that concern the state in general or particular groups with which the administrators are involved.

Coordination Problems and Quality Control. Given the increased interest in research, demands for access to the district's data and research staff outweighed the ability to respond, and concerns about coordination and quality began to emerge. Coordination problems in Los Rios can be summarized as follows:

1. The "Surprise!" problem: Who's saying what about Los Rios, and where?
2. The "They Did It *How?*" problem: How should questionable research methodology, wrong questions, inaccurate data, graphics with no analysis, and incorrect analysis be handled?
3. The "We Want Computer Analysis *Now!*" problem: How can we plan for and coordinate the best use of scarce resources and personnel at both the college and the district level?
4. The "This Study Is the Most Important One" problem: Who sets priorities for use of research staff, computer time, and statistical and written analyses?

The chancellor and the college presidents were primarily concerned about resources, coordination, and quality control. Staffing to handle the increased volume of requests for data and analysis was also a serious problem. The largest of the district's three colleges had long supported an office of research and development, with a key administrator who had research as a partial responsibility and a faculty member who undertook various college-specific studies, often with the assistance of his statistics class (giving his students practical research experience). The other two colleges did not have formal research offices, although several administrators had undertaken and completed widely recognized studies on their own initiative. These two colleges soon requested staffing (or conversion of positions) to support the research function and to coordinate research at the college level. Given the choice between adding staff to the district's Office of Planning and Research and putting staff at each of the colleges to help coordinate, set priorities for, and conduct college-specific research, the presidents and the chancellor elected to add staff at the colleges, thereby creating a district-coordinated (rather than increasingly centralized) model.

Operational Focus: The District Research Council

Each college now had a research office, with someone responsible for research (and for planning, in line with the district model). Clear lines of communication and coordination with the district's director and office of planning and research were needed. The district and the colleges also needed some way of handling problems with coordination, quality control, and data-base access. The District Research Council (DRC) was the answer.

Membership and Role. DRC is composed of the district's director of planning and research, the district's OP&R staff (the district coordinator of research, and a systems software specialist), the college directors of research (and their staff, in two cases—the smallest college has only one person in research), and the director of data processing. DRC's primary role is to provide coordination and quality control and make recommendations on district and college research and data-base priorities.

The need for the college research directors to be part of DRC is clear, but the need to include the director of data processing may not be. Although OP&R has unimpeded access to the district's data base through the systems software specialist (who reports to the director of planning and research), close coordination with the director of data processing is an advantage, particularly as a means of enabling the research staff to have some influence on changes in the structure or functioning of the district's data-gathering and data-reporting systems. In California, moreover, some statewide initiatives entail the requirement to send specific data on tape to the state level, for evaluation of how the initiatives are working. When such tapes are sent directly from the data-processing department, they may or may not contain the specific elements needed for determining how an initiative is functioning at the district or college level. In our experience, communication with the data-processing director is crucial. OP&R does not use the data-processing staff to support its research studies; it has its own systems software specialist, who has access to the mainframe data base. Nevertheless, it is important to coordinate major uses of the computer with the director of data processing, so that computer operations can flow smoothly.

Coordination Lines, Responsibilities, and Strategies. DRC advises the district OP&R director, who in turn advises the chancellor and the cabinet (composed of the chancellor, the college presidents, and other key administrators, including the director of planning and research). Specific coordination lines and responsibilities were developed by the members of DRC, discussed with the chancellor and cabinet, and approved.

The chancellor's cabinet is responsible for approving districtwide research priorities, including allocation of resources; discussing policy implications identified in the research studies; and determining how to implement necessary changes.

The director of OP&R is responsible for making recommendations to the chancellor and the cabinet regarding districtwide research priorities, including analysis of resource needs; providing overall coordination and quality control for all published research in the Los Rios Community College District; maintaining close coordination with data processing, DRC, and the College Offices of Research (COR), a responsibility that includes data-base design and development, research-design assistance, statistical analysis, and prepublication review of studies that have policy implications; identifying policy implications that are based on research findings; and assisting in dissemination of research results, both within the district and statewide.

DRC is responsible for assisting in the design and review phases of districtwide research studies, to enhance the value of this research for college planning and evaluation; advising OP&R about faculty or administrative research proposals that may warrant the district's assistance and technical support; and coordinating information on all current college and district research studies through monthly meetings.

The College Offices of Research are responsible for establishing college research priorities and appropriate review and approval by college administrators; coordinating all college research, including faculty-specific and administrator-specific projects; assisting in design, analysis, and prepublication review of college research; providing computerized analysis, using microcomputer-based software packages, as appropriate; coordinating research activities with DRC and OP&R, particularly projects that require the district's support or have implications for the district's policies; and making recommendations to DRC on districtwide research priorities, including analysis of resource needs, with appropriate review and approval by college administrators.

Faculty- and administrator-specific research requests are reviewed first by the college research office (where priorities are often discussed with the respective college president). Determination of which projects can best be handled by the colleges and which may need the district's support (or may even become districtwide studies) is made right at the college level. If a particular project is a major priority and requires the district's support, the college research director can move it quickly to DRC. The other colleges can learn about it (and perhaps decide to participate), and the district director of OP&R can get an idea of where that project's priority stands with all three colleges. Responsibility for balancing demands from the colleges with those of the chancellor and other district office administrators and for making recommendations to the chancellor's cabinet lies with the district research director. If the cabinet does not agree with or understand a recommendation, it may refuse to allocate resources or may return the request to the director of OP&R and to DRC for reconsideration.

Research Design and Technical Assistance. Key to this model is the focus on district and college research staff members as people who want to encourage and provide technical assistance for research projects. DRC is purposely kept small, so that concerns can be shared and decisions can be made quickly about project support and priorities. Technical assistance takes four major forms: initial research-design assistance, statistical analysis, data downloading, and prepublication review.

Initial research-design assistance, whether done at the college or district level, includes determination of appropriate research or policy questions, analysis of data needs, choice of appropriate methodology, and survey structure and design—in short, advice on how to ask the right questions to get the answers one needs. Statistical analysis at the district level may involve use of statistical packages on the mainframe computer, microcomputer-based analysis or graphics packages, or assistance with using microcomputer-based statistical packages (which each college has in its research office). It also includes, at both levels, advice on designing a study to facilitate computerized statistical analysis, as well as general assistance with statistical information and techniques and consultation on using other statistical software for spreadsheets and graphing. Data downloading generally involves OP&R staff, who do first-pass statistical analyses on the district's mainframe computer, alter the data files for each college (to fit the program that the college wants to use), and put the analyzed files on floppy disks for further use by the college research staff. Prepublication review includes an analysis, at the draft stage of a report, of whether the right questions were asked, the methodology was appropriate, the surveys were structured correctly, and the charts and graphs are clear, to help produce the best possible report and avoid postpublication embarrassment.

Setting Research Agendas

While there is coordination between the colleges and the district office on specific research studies, the ways in which those studies appear on the research agenda at each level may vary. In some cases, interest in doing a particular study is an outgrowth of the district's or college's planning-implementation-evaluation (PIE) process; in others, studies emerge as a result of internal or external forces that influence the agenda and priorities.

District and College PIE Processes. The Los Rios District's PIE process, like its research model, has evolved over the last several years, from a primarily centralized to a more decentralized but coordinated process. Originally, the district office, through the board and the chancellor, established districtwide goals and objectives that the colleges implemented. Great effort was involved in rewriting the objectives every year; college and district staff spent considerable time explaining (in an annual status report) how they had addressed each separate, districtwide goal and objective. The goals themselves were reasonably general, but the different objectives were neither specific nor necessarily important to each college. In fact, the colleges sometimes wrote their own documents, to reflect their own priorities and concerns. Research studies (generally the evaluation phase of a particular objective) became objectives in themselves. District studies often reflected the issues and priorities of districtwide goals and statewide mandates, while the colleges preferred to design and implement evaluation studies that answered their questions about their own objectives.

Given these parallel but not necessarily coherent planning processes, the district and college research agendas were sometimes at odds. The district might feel that it was time to institute evaluation of a particular districtwide initiative; the colleges were often in different phases of implementation or had decided on a different focus for the initiative or, perhaps, had decided not to implement that initiative at all. The upshot was a change in direction for the entire PIE process at both the college and the district level. Henceforth, goals (ten of them) would be set districtwide; objectives would be college-specific. Particular projects or initiatives that clearly had to be coordinated closely with the district office emerged as district office–specific objectives (sometimes with their appropriate counterparts appearing as college objectives). Goals and objectives are now written only every other year, to leave time for implementation and evaluation. The status report is still done annually, but each college reports only on its own specific objectives.

With districtwide goals but flexible, college-specific objectives, priorities for research and evaluation at the college level can reflect the colleges' interests and be reflected in a coherent college-level research agenda. The revised PIE process is now four years old and apparently is working well. There is much more involvement and commitment on the part of college staff. One of the colleges has set the production of a formal college research agenda as a specific objective for the coming two-year planning cycle.

Research Projects and Priorities. The district's research agenda, formally published as the OP&R work plan, includes production of a wide variety of studies, ranging from evaluations of state-funded initiatives to numerous special projects on student transfer, alumni follow-up, enrollment projections, demographic studies, and employment projections needed for development and funding of the district's new college and outreach centers. Some of the more than thirty different projects must await additional staff and other resources.

The college research agendas are less formal but no less extensive. They involve a variety of college-specific projects, including evaluations of state-mandated programs, staff-development initiatives, and classroom-based research studies. Community needs assessments are also planned and implemented, particularly as part of new curriculum- or program-development efforts.

The research agendas at both levels call for standard reports with specific schedules but enough flexibility to accommodate new projects and changing priorities. For example, the need for OP&R to provide enrollment, demographic, and employment projections has meant that some other projects have had to be delayed. Changing politics and priorities are a fact of life for any research office, and the ability to move quickly in responding to new requests is paramount.

Implementing and Monitoring the Research Program

Responsibility for implementing and monitoring the research program in the Los Rios District rests primarily with the college research directors and with the district Office of Planning and Research and its director. Nevertheless, the extent to which college or district research directors and staff are involved in a particular project is directly related to whether that project is seen as college-specific, districtwide, or both.

Districtwide Research. In projects on the districtwide research agenda that address districtwide priorities (such as evaluation of our three transfer centers, our biennial follow-up studies of students, and our program-review data-trends analyses), the district OP&R staff is chiefly responsible for implementing and monitoring the research as it progresses. Project-design responsibility is shared with DRC, particularly in determining the level at which analysis should be done. Projects generally include aggregate analysis of research or evaluation results at the district level, with highlights of differences by college; charts and graphs that match those in the body of the report are done for each college and are included in appendixes. For example, our program-review data-trends project is a districtwide study, with all the results organized by program within each college. The involvement of DRC and college faculty and program staff was crucial to the design, implementation, and evaluation of the study and to the subsequent improvement of the research information for use at the college level.

For a districtwide project, the OP&R staff gathers and analyzes the data and produces the report, drafts of which are sent to DRC for comments. If problems are encountered with data, funding, or some technical area, the OP&R staff attempts to solve them; the district research director may consult the chancellor's cabinet if the need for high-level resolution becomes apparent.

When a new and pressing research project forces delay or cancellation of one or more of the current high-priority projects, the district research director is responsible for recommending which projects to hold. In practice, this decision is often discussed informally with the DRC before a recommendation is made to the chancellor's cabinet.

College-Specific Research. College-specific research may entail major collegewide studies, program-specific evaluations, or classroom-based research conducted by faculty. Given the many types of such research, college research directors have a substantial job monitoring the different research, data-gathering, and quick and dirty analysis projects being conducted on their campuses at any time. While they are responsible for conducting major collegewide studies and specific program evaluations, the college research directors and their staffs may find it difficult to monitor all faculty- or administrator-specific research projects.

The inclusion of specific research projects in the colleges' planning objectives (with particular staff and resources assigned and deadlines set) certainly helps with implementation and monitoring at the college level. In addition, college and district research newsletters help keep everyone informed of what is going on, of where projects are in their development, and of when results will be available for review. Occasionally, faculty members and administrators resent oversight of their research projects. This situation is relatively rare, but it can cause monitoring problems for college research directors and presidents, particularly if sensitive data are involved.

The involvement of college research directors in key campus committees (planning, budgeting, program review, staff development) helps ensure that they hear about and can help direct upcoming or ongoing research. Again, the ability to get faculty and staff involved in research and evaluation design is crucial to implementing the college research agenda.

Results and Implications

The processes for analyzing research results and implications are similar to those for implementing and monitoring research. They vary according to whether college-specific or districtwide research is involved.

District Processes. At the district level, the key people responsible for critical analysis of results and conclusions are the OP&R director and staff. Each of the OP&R staff members is responsible for critically reading the others' studies, at the earliest draft stages (in addition to having been in on the design phase) and as the drafts progress. Additional statistical analyses are often done as new questions arise from the initial results and from OP&R staff members' comments. This process strengthens the studies as they progress and helps provide ideas for presentation and publication strategies.

Since most OP&R research studies are discussed from their inception with DRC, drafts may also be critically reviewed by DRC members. For a study that has a particular program focus (such as the OP&R evaluation of our three colleges' transfer centers), an informal advisory committee is usually established, or a standing committee (such as the one that coordinates the transfer centers' activities districtwide) is used. In our experience, the greater the involvement of program staff and faculty in the evaluation or research project right from the start, the greater the interest in (and commitment to using) the research results.

A number of OP&R studies begin as OP&R unit objectives in the district's PIE process. Once a study or report is completed, it is shared with the chancellor and the cabinet, and then with the board, as part of the evaluation of the program or service involved. Implications for change in either policies or practices are carefully noted in each report and emphasized with key decision makers in the district. Sometimes a study is occasioned by a specific state mandate or policy question, in which case the chancellor may use the results and implications at the statewide policy level.

College Processes. At the college level, the key people responsible for critically analyzing the results of research and the soundness of conclusions are the college research directors, who usually work closely with their presidents. The process varies somewhat at each of our colleges, but most college research involves at least an informal advisory committee (usually composed of program staff and faculty) and key college administrators who are interested in using the results. Review processes occur throughout a project. Results are often shared first, in draft form, with the advisory committee and later, in more polished form, with the college presidents' administrative councils. The college presidents are ultimately responsible for effecting the changes resulting from the implications of college-based research.

Dissemination of Research Results

College and districtwide publication of college research reports occurs frequently, so that staff at all three colleges can be informed of ideas and results. OP&R makes copies and executive summaries of most of its studies available districtwide. The colleges also have various publications in which to highlight research results, including research newsletters (one college even has a special newsletter on classroom-based research), college newspapers, and in-house faculty and staff newsletters.

Some college-based research studies in the Los Rios District have been presented at statewide conferences; others have been published in various statewide media. Support for research has often also meant support for publications and for presentation-related travel. Research results are increasingly linked to institutional effectiveness.

According to its particular emphasis (on vocational education, for example), a study may be shared with occupational-area deans and their faculties, for use in program planning and review. If the study involves the evaluation of a special program or service, particularly one that has been highlighted as a planning objective, it may be published as a formal report and shared not only with the entire campus but also with the district chancellor and the board of trustees through presentation at a board meeting. Such studies are an integral part of the district's PIE process and are often highlighted, with wide distribution of the research report and its executive summary. Staff of the program or project being evaluated are generally also involved in the presentation and usually share their ideas about how the research results will be used at the program level. Whether the process is at the college or the district level, the ability of research results to influence organizational change depends on three things: the quality and clarity of the research and its results, the institutional climate for change, and, most important, the support of the chief executive officer.

The Model in Action

Perhaps the best example of this model of coordinated decentralization is the district's series of student follow-up studies, which began as a state-mandated compliance report and have developed into the collection of college-, pro-gram-, and skills-specific information used for planning and evaluation.

In 1983, the Los Rios District, like most other California districts, was involved in follow-up of vocational students, primarily as a result of state mandates for compliance with federal Vocational Education Data System (VEDS) reporting requirements. Once the new research office was estab-lished, a new follow-up study for vocational students was initiated, one that would meet district as well as state and federal needs.

The 1983 report was designed with the help of the colleges' three occupational education deans. At the design stage, their primary desire was to have a better way of handling the follow-up procedures, so that the VEDS compliance report would be easier to do. OP&R wanted to undertake a pilot study that would meet the needs of the compliance report but also provide pertinent information, not only on the success of our vocational students but also on their opinions of particular district and college ser-vices. Questionnaires and data-processing services of the Center for Infor-mation Services (of the Tex-SIS system) were used. Over 2,700 students were surveyed, and an adjusted response rate of 51.8 percent was achieved, which was far above the usual response rates for the VEDS survey. Several innovations—typesetting of the survey, inclusion of a special letter from the chancellor, structuring of the questionnaire so that the student-opinion questions came first and employment and salary data came later, and inclusion of a space for open-ended comments—probably contributed to the higher return rate. The report was presented to the board, as well as to others in various district settings, where it was well received.

The review process for the pilot report included the deans of occupa-tional education and DRC. Three major changes were made as a result of this review: a single composite questionnaire was designed, to better reflect the needs of the Los Rios district and its colleges (the pilot had used separate and slightly different survey forms for graduates and nongradu-ates); the survey population was expanded to include all (not just voca-tional) graduates and certificate earners; and data analysis was done on the district's mainframe computer with SPSS-X, rather than through a con-tract with the Tex-SIS personnel. The next two years' surveys and reports supported the idea that the changes were stimulating more interest in the research and its implications. The chancellor, the board members, the presidents, and, particularly, the deans of occupational education were delighted that the responses from students were so positive. The results of the studies even found their way to the state legislature, where our finding that the many nonreturning students were not dropouts but quite successful "dropins" had a major impact on the state-level debate about the sup-posedly high drop-out rate in community colleges.

In 1986, we again met with the deans of occupational education and, later, with DRC members, to determine what else we could do to get the results used where they really mattered—in the classroom. The DRC members and the deans, after consultation with college faculty, finally told us the one thing that we needed to hear: most faculty were really only concerned about their own program areas, and we needed to somehow get the data to the program-specific (not just college-specific) level. As a result, the spring 1986 follow-up study organized survey responses from the same questionnaire in a different format. Program-specific summaries were prepared for each program receiving ten or more student responses, along with totals for each college and for the district as a whole. The program-level data were produced in a special four-page format designed for quick reading and easy use. The new format was successful in enabling the colleges' faculty and area deans to use the information in program-review efforts. Assistance from the college research directors was crucial in working with college faculty and staff. Turnaround time for the spring survey results was dramatically shortened, to provide the data in time for use in fall program review and spring program development. Presentations at the college and work with program area staff helped get the results used by those who could make the necessary changes.

The recommendations of college staff and those of DRC members resulted in even more enhancements for the spring 1989 survey. For that survey, a one-page, program-specific questionnaire was added to the regular questionnaire packet, so that data about particular skills learned and needed in the workplace could be compared to data on classes taken. The fact that DRC members and their research office staffs assisted with the survey mailout and data collection, as well as with the program areas' faculty in getting the research results used, is testimony that what was once a district-office compliance report has become an integral part of getting student follow-up and response information back to those who can use it to make a difference. Finally, at every step of the way, we enjoyed support from the chancellor and the college presidents.

Strengths and Weaknesses of the Model

The progression from a centralized research model to one of coordinated decentralization in the Los Rios District can be viewed as a result of increasing support for and interest in research throughout the district or as a result of college autonomy in a multicampus district. To a considerable extent, both of these viewpoints are accurate. The quality of research has improved, at both the district and the college level. Whether it would have done so if the centralized approach had remained, and if staff had been added to the district research office, is certainly arguable. The strengths and weaknesses of the model depend on the perspective from which judgment is made—the colleges' or the district's.

The District Perspective: Too Many Cooks? From the district perspective, as the model currently functions, there are more strengths than weaknesses. OP&R and college research office studies alike benefit from the shared ideas and combined talents of a wider group of researchers. In addition, the college research offices are closer to the customer (students and faculty) and can provide insights into how to make a study and its results more meaningful at the college level (as in the case of our student follow-up studies). Moreover, the district research office, with its orientation toward evaluation and policy, can assist the college researchers with ideas on how to coordinate our research for both local and eventual statewide policy impact in areas of particular concern to Los Rios (and often to other districts). Finally, the mutual respect and commitment to good research and to making a difference, shared by researchers at both levels, help keep the model functioning in a far less formal manner than might otherwise be the case.

The one possibly serious threat to this model lies in the desire of people throughout the district to have direct access to the district's mainframe data base—and for a variety of reasons. Such requests must now come through the college research offices and DRC, primarily because access to the data base involves writing sophisticated computer programs, but the new computer system may change that. The current query function is primarily a programming tool in data processing, for quick retrieval of data files. On the horizon, however, is a more user-friendly version of the query program, which may provide access to slices of the data base from virtually any terminal in the district.

The concerns about quality control, research coordination, and database access that DRC and the model were intended to solve may again rear their heads as serious problems. The advent of too many cooks into the research kitchen could bring back all the old problems, but on a far larger scale. Research is and should be a painstaking process that involves thorough review and analysis before results are shared or used widely. The possibility of almost anyone—including people without research skills and awareness of caveats and policy implications—being able to use the district's data base to turn out charts, graphs, and quick and dirty analyses is one that could threaten the continued existence of the current model. The technology is there to make this scenario possible. Whether DRC and OP&R, working together with all concerned, can make the continued decentralization of research responsibilities a positive situation remains to be seen.

The College Perspective: Too Much Control? In the multicampus coordinated research model, individual colleges' priorities must compete, and not everything can be done. This is clearly a problem for the individual colleges, but the strength of this situation lies in the cooperative basis of decisions about which research projects will have top priority and claim relatively scarce staff, time, computer support, and funding. It is also guaranteed that a number of people must review and approve any research project before it can be realized. That can be a benefit, in terms of quality control, but it may also be a liability, in terms of getting a project started and finished quickly.

The ability of a college president to request and quickly receive a research report that involves more than just the data readily available at the college is sometimes hampered by the DRC coordination process and by the inability of the district's small research staff to respond as quickly as would be hoped. (Generally speaking, requests from the chancellor are accorded top priority in the district OP&R, and so the coordination process does not appear so daunting at the district level.) Moreover, some college research staff bridle at the ability of the district office to say yes or no to a particular research effort (although this generally does not happen without substantial consultation). The strong sentiments for college autonomy in the Los Rios District (and probably in many other multicampus districts) provide a creative tension about control that affects not only research but also all areas of the district and the colleges. In most cases, this tension is healthy and results in better education and wiser expenditure of public funds.

The Los Rios District's research model is one that has evolved over time and will probably continue to change. A new chancellor, new technology, or new research personnel could all result in a somewhat different model over the next several years. From the point of view of the current research staff, the administration, and, certainly, the board, the model works. The research itself (and the ways it is received by those inside and beyond the district) will continue to provide the best measures of this model's success.

Reference

Coffey, J. C. *Proving What We're Doing Is Working: The Student Flow Research Model.* Sacramento, Calif.: Los Rios Community College District, 1987. (ED 279 379)

Janis Cox Jones (formerly Coffey) is director of planning and research for the Los Rios Community College District, Sacramento, California. She worked eight years for the California Postsecondary Education Commission and recently took a ten-month leave to coauthor the state's reassessment study of the California Community Colleges.

*The decentralized institutional research model is a means of
conducting practical, change-oriented research and inculcating
a research-evaluation perspective among all professional staff.*

The Decentralized Research Model

*Peter R. MacDougall, Jack Friedlander, Elaine Cohen,
John Romo*

Santa Barbara City College (SBCC) is a comprehensive community college
that serves over 11,000 students in its credit programs and an additional
33,000 in its noncredit division. The college enjoys a reputation in California as a leader in the production of meaningful institutional research.

Before 1984, the assistant to the president was responsible for college
planning, grant development, and administrative data processing. An evaluation of the college's research program revealed that much of the research
effort was spent gathering data and preparing reports for external agencies.
Research for internal campus use was limited to occasional needs assessments, surveys, program evaluations, and the production of an annual
college atlas documenting institutional and departmental trends.

The results of the evaluation revealed that few members of the college
staff were aware of the research studies being conducted; that only a handful
of faculty and staff were involved in the studies; that the reports being
generated did not address the primary concerns of line managers or faculty
and, as a result, were often not read; and that few saw the direct connection
between the studies being conducted by the staff responsible for institutional
research and the improvement of instructional and support programs.

In an effort to ensure that institutional research was integrated into
the ongoing operation of the college's instructional and support programs,
the college president formed an institutional research committee. This
committee, composed of line managers and faculty, was given the responsibility of coordinating research activities directly related to college operations. Research responsibilities pertaining to the preparation of state- and
federally mandated reports, as well as to the maintenance of the integrity

of the college's data bases and management information system, remained with the assistant to the president. This approach to institutional research is called the *decentralized research model.*

Description of the Model

Philosophy. The decentralized research model is an alternative to the traditional organizational structure for institutional research found in most community colleges. In this model, research and evaluation are perceived as being essential to institutional effectiveness. A broad-based approach to evaluation is sought, and all staff have roles to fulfill in this important college function. The model reflects the long-term objective of having teaching and administrative staff involved with and competent in evaluation efforts that will enhance the college's ability to deliver high-quality educational programs and services. Specifically, instructors are encouraged to assess the effectiveness of various teaching strategies, and managers and staff members are asked to improve results by assessing changes that can be made in their areas.

The decentralized model is seen as an excellent means of achieving the objective of making institutional research the responsibility of all staff. It was selected over the traditional approach—an office of institutional research (or of planning and research)—because of the concern that an office of institutional research would be perceived as the only place where research was conducted and as the only office responsible for institutional research.

The model is based on the following principles:

1. The purpose of institutional research is to increase institutional effectiveness by improving the teaching and learning environment.
2. All levels of management have a commitment to institutional research.
3. All professional staff are to be involved in institutional research and evaluation.
4. Institutional research should support staff and institutional development.
5. Collaborative efforts among staff in different areas of the college are encouraged.
6. The responsibility for research is to be distributed among staff members from the major organizational components and levels of the college.
7. Research results are to be applied to improving the college's programs.

Thus, the decentralized research model demonstrates and enhances the value of the teacher or administrator as researcher and seeks to integrate this value into the college's culture.

Major Functions. The model consists of seven activities: to determine research objectives; to establish processes and responsibilities for conducting the research; to monitor research projects; to identify research results and draw conclusions; to determine institutional changes to be effected; to disseminate results to college groups (divisions, departments, committees, trustees); and to evaluate the outcomes of institutional research.

Staff Involved in Institutional Research

The institutional research program at SBCC is conducted by a committee, rather than by a manager responsible for this function. The committee is composed of two deans of instruction, with line responsibilities for academic programs; the assistant dean of admissions and records; a counselor; the assistant to the president, who serves as an administrative liaison to the data-processing center; and a faculty member of the mathematics department, who is well versed in data-base management. The members of the committee are appointed by the college president, in consultation with the vice-president for academic affairs and the vice-president for student affairs. Appointments are based on the candidates' interest in research and ability to represent major organizational areas of the college. The vice-presidents for academic and student affairs and the college president are significantly involved in the college research function.

Role of the CEO. The college president sets the tone for the emphasis placed on conducting and applying institutional research. This model, in particular, places the president in a leadership-coordinating role, through which she or he is integrally involved in establishing the college's research philosophy, identifying the research agenda, monitoring the progress of projects, identifying institutional changes to be effected, and disseminating results. What is most significant, the president provides leadership, supporting the institutional changes that will result from effective research efforts, and provides the visibility that institutional research requires for integration into the college's culture.

Role of the Vice-Presidents. In the decentralized model, the vice-presidents for academic and student affairs have several of their staff members involved in the research effort, as members of the institutional research committee or as participants in carrying out specific projects. The vice-presidents are responsible for facilitating and monitoring the efforts of their staff assigned to carry out the studies. The vice-presidents establish an environment supportive of research activities, participate directly in establishing the research agenda, provide the staff time and resources required to complete assigned projects, determine from research results the institutional changes to be made, disseminate results, and evaluate the costs and benefits of institutional research efforts.

Role of the Deans. The deans of academic and student affairs are the hub of this research model. They have primary responsibility for carrying out the research projects, as well as major responsibility in all other research activities. Their responsibility for institutional research is assumed as complementary to their leadership and management functions.

Role of Other Committee Members. The assistant to the president provides a direct link between the president's office and the institutional research committee and serves as administrative liaison to the data-processing center. The counselor represents the interests of the counseling department, which is very active in institutional research. The math instructor is involved with the college's assessment program and provides a direct link to it. These individuals participate in all activities of the institutional research committee.

Role of the Data-Processing Director. All requests for access to the mainframe computer are reviewed by the institutional research committee and the data-processing center's manager. The statistical analyses for a particular project are determined by the institutional research committee, in consultation with the data-processing director, when the project is conceptualized. Issues pertaining to the use and confidentiality of data and to the length of time the information can be used are reviewed before access is granted. In addition to protecting the confidentiality of data on college students and staff, this review protects the college from using different sets of information to address the same question. Studies that do not involve information residing in the mainframe computer are conducted by the institutional research committee independently of the data-processing center.

The Research Agenda

The initial draft of the research agenda is developed by members of the institutional research committee. Many of the items included in the agenda result from interactions among members of the committee, staff in their departments, and senior administrators. The draft of the agenda is reviewed by the college president, the vice-presidents for academic and student affairs, and other members of the institutional research committee. This review usually takes the form of a discussion, in which institutional values and strategic directions of the college provide the context for evaluating the proposed agenda and reaching consensus on its contents.

The primary criterion for selecting items to be included in the institutional research agenda is potential for answering questions that determine the direction of some aspect of the college's program. Other criteria involve practical considerations. Is there expertise to carry out the study? Is staff time available to complete tasks? Is there funding? Can data-processing requirements be met? How important is the project, by comparison with others?

A representative from the college's data-processing center attends meetings to assist in planning the research agenda. Proposed projects are reviewed by the data-processing manager, who provides estimates on the programming time needed to complete tasks. The amount of programming time required is included in the cost estimate for completing the project. This factor, along with the expected benefits of the project, is taken into account by the committee and senior administrators.

The agenda is forwarded to the college's planning council for review and comment, and it is shared with other appropriate college committees. Ultimately, consensus on the research agenda is reached by the institutional research committee, the vice-presidents, and the president.

Members of the institutional research committee are assigned specific projects, to be carried out in their respective areas. Studies in specific areas are conducted by committee members and others. The committee also establishes timelines, research procedures, and costs.

Monitoring the Research Projects

The members of the institutional research committee meet during the year to monitor the progress of the studies and to identify the results and implications of the research. Committee members assist one another in formulating the design of the studies, selecting appropriate survey instruments, evaluating the soundness of the results and recommendations identified from the research, and critiquing the reports prepared to disseminate the research findings. Noncommittee members involved in carrying out a particular research project are required to attend any institutional research committee meetings where their projects are reviewed.

The vice-presidents monitor research by ensuring that the research activities are consistent with the project objectives and are addressing issues directly related to the quality of the institution's programs and services; evaluating whether projects are consistent with established timelines, resources, and commitments of staff time; identifying research findings that have direct implications for programs; and keeping all staff members and the college president informed of progress in the research effort.

Since institutional research represents only a portion of any administrator's or faculty member's assignment, it is particularly important that the vice-presidents monitor this activity, to ensure that balance is maintained between the time administrators spend on research and the time they devote to the remainder of their administrative assignments. This is a particular concern in this model because all staff involved in the research effort also have major management or teaching responsibilities.

At the end of each academic year, the college president meets with the two vice-presidents, members of the institutional research committee, administrators, and faculty involved in the research. The purpose of this half-day meeting is to evaluate the effectiveness of the research effort by the following criteria: satisfactory completion of projects; involvement of college staff in the projects; extensiveness of the dissemination of findings;

significance of the research implications for improving institutional effectiveness; and significance of the changes in institutional practices that have resulted or will result from research. The information reviewed in this meeting, along with the institutional objectives for the upcoming year, is taken into account in the formulation of the next year's research agenda.

Identifying Results and Implications

In addition to holding many informal discussions with faculty and staff, members of the institutional research committee meet with the college president and vice-presidents at least four times per year, to review the findings and implications of the research studies. Before these meetings, the chair of the institutional research committee prepares a report on the status of each project with respect to its progress, findings, and implications for institutional improvement. The report also contains a section on institutional practices that have been altered as a result of the research. During these meetings, decisions are made about the degree to which the objectives of the studies are being achieved, adjustments to be made in the research agenda, soundness of the conclusions drawn from the research, and institutional changes to be made as a result of the research. The vice-presidents identify the findings that have direct implications for their programs and take the lead in strengthening those programs.

Determining Implications for College Practices

The processes followed in this model are designed to integrate institutional research into the ongoing development of the college. A unique feature of this approach is that senior administrators of the college are directly involved in all phases of the research effort. As a result, throughout the monitoring of projects and assessment of results, they consistently seek to establish the relationship between research results and the potential for change in institutional practices. At the annual meeting of the institutional research committee, the vice-presidents, and the president, considerable time is spent evaluating the institutional changes to be considered or made as a consequence of the research findings. Recommendations are either implemented immediately or subjected to governance processes, whereby the research-based reasons for changes are explained, as a way of developing support.

Dissemination of Findings and Recommendations

Members of the institutional research committee are responsible for discussing results and recommendations with the vice-presidents, faculty, and staff in their respective areas. For example, the deans of instruction include research reports as an agenda item at most of their division and departmental meetings. Dissemination of research findings takes place during all phases of a study and provides faculty and staff an opportunity to discuss potential implications for areas in which they have direct responsibility, as well as for the college.

The vice-presidents also discuss research results and implications with their staffs. These meetings are an excellent forum for disseminating the findings to staff members who are not directly involved in the research and for discussing the implications of the findings. Having all line managers involved in dissemination has increased participation in and support of the institutional research program.

Results and implications of the studies are disseminated through written reports, prepared by members of the committee responsible for a particular project, and through oral reports made to members of divisions, departments, and support services. Committee members also discuss the studies at weekly staff meetings chaired by their respective vice-presidents. Reports are also routinely presented to the board of trustees.

Advantages and Disadvantages of the Model

The strengths and weaknesses discussed here have been identified through the experiences of the authors and discussions with institutional researchers throughout the country.

Advantages

1. A greater number of staff members than in the traditional model are directly involved in the development, implementation, and evaluation of the research program. This broad-based participation allows for the development of staff interest and expertise in institutional research.

2. The decentralized model allows for direct involvement of line administrators and staff members in all phases of the research process, from identification of research questions to analysis of findings and recommendations, dissemination of findings, and development of strategies for implementing recommendations.

3. The direct involvement of line managers and staff members, either through membership on the institutional research committee or discussions of the research strategies, heightens their disposition to accept and adopt recommendations based on the research projects.

4. The frequent contact of line managers who are responsible for institutional research with faculty and staff in their areas of responsibility provides them with a realistic view of the importance of the studies, the appropriateness of the procedures for data collection, the soundness of the findings, and the practicality of the recommendations drawn from the research studies.

5. There is a savings associated with this model in that the college does not have to hire additional personnel to staff an institutional research office.

Disadvantages

1. Not having one individual responsible for the research function may mean that no one person is accountable for seeing that the research agenda is implemented appropriately and in a timely manner.

2. Since institutional research is only one of the committee members' responsibilities, there may be a tendency toward slower analysis of project findings.

3. Committee members may demonstrate a tendency to become too involved in research, at the expense of their core functions. A successful research effort may expand research activities, and these may detract from fulfillment of other responsibilities.

4. Since the members of the institutional research committee are selected from among existing staff, the committee may lack an individual with expertise in research design, measurement, and statistics. Line managers responsible for the institutional research program may also lack the time to acquire greater levels of expertise in research or to keep abreast of developments in the field.

5. Using line managers and members of particular departments introduces the potential for bias in program evaluation.

Application of the Model

Determining Research Objectives. Since 1983, the college has made a substantial investment in its comprehensive matriculation program, designed to help all newly matriculated students achieve their educational objectives. It was expected that, since the college had been making improvements in the process each year, the matriculation program would see steady gains in retention, persistence, and program completion. On the basis of the importance of the assumed gains in this program, the institutional research committee identified the evaluation of the matriculation program as the top priority. This priority was confirmed in a meeting with the president and vice-presidents.

Establishing Processes and Responsibilities. Responsibility for evaluating the matriculation program was assigned to the chair of the institutional research committee, a dean of academic affairs who had not been closely involved in the development of the program and could therefore bring objectivity to the evaluation. A software program was written to provide analyses of the longitudinal data necessary for the evaluation. The programming provided the ability to generate the necessary semester reports for retention, academic progress, and persistence of matriculated students, from fall 1983 to the current semester.

Monitoring the Project. The project was monitored by the president, the vice-presidents, and the matriculation committee, as well as by the institutional research committee, which reviewed preliminary findings and made recommendations for additional information to be provided. The reports were reviewed and critiqued by the institutional research committee before being presented to the vice-presidents, the president, and the rest of the college community.

Identifying Research Results. Findings from the longitudinal study of performance and persistence among newly matriculated students included the following:

1. There was a steady increase in semester-to-semester persistence rates of newly matriculated students who entered the college from 1983 to 1988.
2. Among students in the matriculation program, 90 percent had followed advice provided by counselors regarding course selection.
3. Approximately 30 percent of the students who had been expected to participate avoided doing so by enrolling during the late-registration period.
4. Students who participated in the program were more likely to persist than students who did not.
5. Full-time students were much more likely than part-time students to complete a greater percentage of their courses with a grade of C or higher and to reenroll in college the second semester.

Similar findings resulted for day and evening students. Ethnicity of students was not a discriminating factor on percentage of units completed with a grade of C or better, first-to-second-semester persistence, and first-to-third-semester persistence. The evaluation demonstrated that the college's investment of resources in its matriculation program was warranted. Although the results were positive, it was clear that students in the first semester, even those who were prepared for college-level work, withdrew from about 25 percent to 35 percent of their courses and that part-time students and late registrants completed only 50 percent of the units they attempted. It became obvious to the research committee that factors beyond test scores and advising affected students' success.

Disseminating Results. The preliminary findings and recommendations were discussed at length with the president and the vice-presidents and were disseminated widely because of the importance of matriculation to the college. The findings were presented to the matriculation committee, the academic senate, the division chair council, the English and math divisions, and the board of trustees, as well as to statewide community college conferences, and an article was published in the faculty newsletter. As a result, new insights have been gained, and additional questions have been raised that will be investigated in the future.

Impact of Results on Policies and Programs. The institutional research committee reviewed and discussed the results of the preliminary evaluation of matriculation and made its recommendations to the president, the vice-presidents, and matriculation committee:

Recommendation. The college should take steps to ensure that all newly matriculated students participate in the assessment, advisement, and orientation program. The late-registration period should be reduced from three weeks to two weeks, and students who enroll late should be required to be advised and assessed.

Action. Changes in institutional practices included developing computer checks, to identify students who had not been assessed and advised, and reducing the late-registration period from three weeks to two.

Recommendation. Effective classroom and counseling strategies should be developed, to increase course completion and persistence among matriculated students and evening-only students, as well as among students who enroll during the late-registration period.

Action. The president, the vice-presidents, and the institutional research committee determined that a major objective for 1988–89 would be the implementation of classroom research projects to increase students' success. In addition, a "college success" course was formulated for entering students.

Determining Research Objectives. The findings from the evaluation of the matriculation program were translated into new research objectives for the next year. These included evaluation of the effectiveness of classroom research projects to improve retention and performance, a study of the effects of the late-registration policy on student retention, and an evaluation of the effectiveness of the new "college success" course on retention and persistence of first-time students.

That the new research objectives were based on the findings from a previous project illustrates the circular nature of this model. The evaluation of the matriculation program further illustrates the assumption (stated at the beginning of this chapter) that the purpose of institutional research is to increase institutional effectiveness by improving programs and services.

Conclusion

The decentralized research model is a means of conducting practical, change-oriented research while inculcating a research-evaluation perspective in the college community. With respect to the model's strengths and weaknesses, the necessity of having staff with enough research competence to fulfill complex responsibilities while still carrying out their primary leadership and management functions is both the primary requisite and the chief difficulty. As applied in one institution, the model has been effective in broadening the base of staff members involved in the research process, increasing the scope of the research effort, and effecting institutional changes that will increase the probability of students' success.

Peter R. MacDougall is president of Santa Barbara City College.

Jack Friedlander is dean of academic affairs at Santa Barbara City College.

Elaine Cohen is dean of academic affairs at Santa Barbara City College.

John Romo is vice-president for academic affairs at Santa Barbara City College.

Elements of the centralized and decentralized institutional research models are combined to address the research needs of a medium-size community college.

The Centralized-Decentralized Research Model

Marylin Orton

Allan Hancock Joint Community College District is a single-campus district in a semirural area along the California coast. The college has an enrollment of approximately six thousand full-time-equivalent students. It enjoys a reputation for progressive educational programming and has a long history of collegiality and cooperation among students, faculty, administrators, and the board of trustees. This type of atmosphere promotes the implementation of new ideas in response to institutional needs.

The need for institutional research became evident when, as a result of the development of a new and sophisticated data base, a flood of statistical reports became available, describing the student body, academic offerings, grade distributions, and a variety of other services and programs on campus. Clearly, there was a need to screen the massive amount of information, analyze the findings, and produce comparative reports.

Another motivation for creating an organized research function on campus was the fact that swings in enrollment were making the planning and scheduling of classes each semester increasingly difficult. In some semesters, large numbers of classes had to be canceled; in others, instructional deans were scrambling to open more sections. Some method for monitoring historical data on the success of offering classes at various times was needed, as was a program to project growth trends. Evaluators within and outside the college were also continually requesting reports and data. Information for self-study, accreditation, program review, and program audits was required on a regular basis. This need has continued to grow as state demands for accountability have increased.

The advent of a state-mandated program for student assessment and retention required validation of assessment instruments, monitoring of matriculated students, follow-up of high-risk students, and evaluation of the entire process. Finally, research data and analysis were essential for overall institutional planning, to evaluate the effectiveness of course offerings and other educational services as well as to guide policy and decisions.

The college initially responded to these needs for institutional research by reassigning a math instructor to serve as an institutional researcher for 60 percent of his contract. The agenda was partly defined by the researcher, who, as a faculty member, knew of many questions that needed to be asked about the instructional program. A series of meetings with the president and members of the administrative team also helped identify other collegewide research needs. A data base was created by the researcher to address the research needs.

Because of growing demands for research studies from almost every segment of the campus, the president appointed a broad-based committee to serve as a steering committee for institutional research. A primary role of this committee was to provide guidance and protection to the researcher. This arrangement ultimately resulted in the development of a centralized-decentralized research model.

Description of the Model

In addressing its institutional research needs, the college recognized the strengths and weaknesses of the centralized and the decentralized research models. It was determined that a combination of the two would best serve the needs of a college the size of Allan Hancock, with the personnel and resources available to it. The centralization was achieved by having the major research goals, projects, and activities identified through the annual review of collegewide objectives and by having one person designated as responsible for centralized institutional research. The decentralization was achieved by creation of a broad-based campus research committee.

The committee was designed not only to represent all areas of the campus but also to draw on the interests and expertise of its members, to form a strong foundation for the development and implementation of a campuswide institutional research program. The committee is composed of faculty members and administrators who have research backgrounds. Current members include a sociology instructor, a math instructor, and a research librarian. Faculty members were invited to serve on the committee by the college president because of their expertise. The academic senate formally appointed these members once they had agreed to serve. Administrative members include the associate dean for student support services, the vice-president for instruction, and the director of computing services. Inclusion of the data-processing administrator is necessary to facilitate communications regarding data availability and competing priorities in the computing center. The involvement of data-processing staff in research, through this committee, provides a vital communications link.

Role of the Committee

Defining the Research Objectives. The campus researcher meets with the committee monthly. The primary task is to create and monitor the research agenda for the college with input from the campus at large.

The research agenda is developed through multiple means. Each fall semester, instructional and student services staff are asked by the president to submit a list of the accomplishments for the prior year, as well as goals for the coming year. This process requires identification of outcome measures once a goal or objective is established. The research needs that are identified through this process are then elicited from each department, through the use of a simple form that addresses objectives and outcome measures sought and asks for a brief description of the proposed study.

Institutionwide research requirements are also determined by the president and the cabinet on the basis of federal and state mandates and total college needs, as identified through annual adoption of the district's goals and objectives. These include ongoing projects and data collection. The campus researcher reviews requests from campus departments and presents them to the committee. All research functions must go through the committee, to ensure that the research priorities of the college are maintained. This review process not only identifies projects that need support but also screens out requests that may be trivial or inappropriate.

Studies are approved according to their relevance to collegewide planning, evaluation of programs, and state mandates. Projects that affect the campus the most, or that address immediate problems or decision-making needs, receive priority. Once all projects are reviewed and priorities are set, timelines for completion are established for each project.

Establishing Procedures and Responsibilities. Primary responsibility to carry out the research agenda lies with the campus researcher, but individual committee members also administer some projects that reflect their areas of expertise, or a subcommittee may carry forward a project, as necessary. For example, a subcommittee interested in persistence and retention recently studied fall-cohort groups for each of five years and tracked their persistence across five semesters. Members also looked at grade distributions and withdrawal rates, by discipline, and at various student characteristics. The research design was presented to the entire committee, and members' suggestions were included. The subcommittee proceeded to conduct the study and present the findings to the entire committee, for comments on the data analysis and a decision on how to disseminate the findings.

In some cases, the committee merely monitors projects carried on in student affairs or instruction and helps interpret and disseminate the information. For example, a need to determine the actual transfer rate of the college led to such a study. While state universities in California provide data on transfers to their feeder institutions, community colleges typically have no way of tracking admission of their students to private and out-of-state institutions. To address this concern, the admissions and counseling offices are gathering data on transfer students by following up transcript requests with letters to the four-year institutions, to see if the students actually enrolled. The numbers will be compared to the number of students who indicated transfer as a goal, in order to determine a more accurate transfer rate. The committee supported the research and ensured that the campus researcher was available to offer advice, but the project was conducted by student services staff.

Suggesting Research Methodologies. Even a professional researcher can use help in designing the best methodology to test a particular hypothesis. Once the research questions are defined and priorities are set, the researcher suggests a methodology, and the committee is invited to comment and make suggestions. Likewise, clarification of research findings and their interpretation can be enhanced if several people have an opportunity to look at the data and assist with the analysis. For example, an elaborate mailout survey on students' satisfaction with summer course offerings was planned because of an apparent change in enrollment patterns. The committee suggested a simple six-question survey to be filled out on a Scantron form in a representative sample of classes. The study was completed, and the results were available within a month. This quick response allowed the college to use the results for identifying new student populations and planning the upcoming schedule, in response to students' needs, as reflected in the survey.

Identifying Resources. In addition to being actively involved in creating the research agenda and providing staff support to the committee, the researcher is responsible for identifying the resources needed to complete any given project. For example, if a particular study will require one hundred hours of data entry and fifty hours of computer programming, the campus researcher must bring these needs to the attention of the committee.

The researcher makes the initial suggestions on the best methodology for addressing a particular research question. Technical expertise most often comes from the researcher, and committee members rely on his sense of how long it will take and how complex it will be to complete a particular project. After the study is outlined and necessary resources are obtained, the project is left in the hands of the researcher, along with a timeline. He interacts with computing services for necessary support. Since the director of computing services is on the committee, most needs have already been identified during the committee meetings. If the researcher has problems with the design or in gathering data, members of the committee are available to help and suggest alternative methods.

Facilitating Specific Research. Recent literature has illustrated the usefulness of simple studies in the classroom, to measure learning outcomes and assess the success of various teaching strategies. By funding selected requests, Allan Hancock College encourages instructors to conduct classroom research. One of the faculty members on the committee has special interest and expertise in classroom research and serves as a research consultant to faculty interested in conducting studies. A professional development committee sponsors instructional-improvement grants, which provide support for a variety of activities, including classroom research. The research committee has been asked to review proposals and issue minigrants to aid instructors in conducting these classroom research projects.

Monitoring Progress. The committee meets monthly, to monitor ongoing and specific research projects, discuss reports of completed studies, and review requests for research and minigrants. The meetings consist of updates to the committee on the status of the research projects. The campus researcher chairs the committee meetings and develops the agenda for each meeting.

When a project is completed, the researcher or the committee member in charge of the study writes a preliminary analysis of the findings. This draft and raw data are distributed to committee members for their review and comments in advance of the next meeting. The content and format are discussed at the committee meeting, and the final report is drafted with input from the committee. The committee is responsible for determining that the report is clear and concise, free of jargon, and easily interpretable by those with limited knowledge of statistics.

Use of Research Results

One of the most frustrating aspects of institutional research is that staff often do not see any results from research efforts because results do not get into the hands of those who need to see them. For example, a study may indicate the need for a change in the curriculum of a particular course, to improve the success rate of a special group of students. If the instructors who teach the course do not see the study or understand its findings, then the research really has no impact on the success of the course or on the students.

The dissemination of findings is the most critical element of the process, and this is a key role of the committee. Distribution may take place at department meetings and committee meetings or in the president's cabinet meetings. The committee, with guidance from the vice-president for instruction, determines the dissemination policy to be followed for each report. Reports are also shared with neighboring community colleges or with colleges involved in similar research.

A research newsletter is published each semester and summarizes the research activities of the committee. It also serves as a forum for faculty to share findings from their classroom research or from research conducted within their own disciplines. Faculty whose work has been published may also be acknowledged in this forum, as may recipients of research mini-grants. The newsletter provides the opportunity to make research findings widely known throughout the campus community, as well as providing information on grants, conferences, and useful journal articles. In regard to more specialized studies, the committee determines the appropriate forum for sharing the results. Results are typically shared with the departments and administrators most affected by the studies.

Research and Policymaking

The results of a research study often have a direct impact on policy and curriculum. For example, last spring a tracking study of remedial English students indicated that attrition was very high among students in a particular course and that very few of them were moving on to the next level of English. Through an analysis of student-background data, the population enrolled in the course was closely examined. It was discovered that the classes were composed largely of economically disadvantaged students, many of whom had participated in noncredit and credit English as a Second Language classes, and of older students, who had dropped out of public secondary schools before graduating. This finding indicated special needs for additional support, study-skills instruction, and confidence-building techniques for these students. After a committee member met with the department, a special task force was created. This group met regularly for the entire semester and redesigned the curriculum to incorporate reading, speaking, writing, and study skills into the course. Class size was also decreased, class length was increased, and peer tutors and counselors were added to the classroom. Pre- and posttests were administered, and the students were tracked after a semester in the newly revised course. Preliminary results indicated a much better retention rate than in previous years, with many more students enrolling in the next level of English. Thus, research was the catalyst in bringing about a positive change for these students.

Institutional research allows college leaders to plan effectively for the changing needs of the college. For example, semester-to-semester comparisons of enrollment data indicated a downward trend, particularly among certain populations. Projections clearly indicated that unless new audiences were attracted to the college, enrollment would continue to decline. It appeared that transferring university students, agricultural workers, and parents of school-age children were unable to begin classes before Labor Day. The cabinet reviewed these findings, along with needs surveys, and planned a change in the academic calendar, to delay the start of fall classes until after Labor Day and to encourage enrollment among the targeted populations.

Research is tied to planning in such areas as establishing and monitoring faculty load, determining staffing needs, and justifying building projects. The vice-president for instruction serves on the committee and provides the direct link with the president and other senior administrators. The president reviews all research reports and regularly shares findings and trends with the board of trustees. When policy changes are recommended by staff, relevant research is used to support the proposals. The connection between research and planning continues to develop as the model evolves.

Examples of Research

Essentially, there are two types of research projects: ongoing and special. The campus researcher conducts ongoing projects relatively independently of the committee. Ongoing projects include analysis of enrollment trends and enrollment projections, descriptions of student-body characteristics and student course loads, campus-to-campus enrollment comparisons, and breakdown of enrollment by zip code, as well as such reports as grade distribution by class, instructor, and discipline. These reports are completed every semester and analyzed in depth by the researcher before being distributed to administrators, department chairs, and instructors. The ongoing reports allow comparisons each semester against baseline data collected over the past eight years.

Special projects are designed to respond to more specific needs. For example, in the Language Arts Department, there had been an ongoing debate about the relative effectiveness of two different English courses in preparing students for freshman composition. Most department members voiced the opinion that one of the courses was inadequate. A study was proposed by the department and approved by the research committee to compare the success of students coming from each of these courses by monitoring their performance in freshman composition. It was found that the common wisdom in the department was incorrect; in fact, students coming from the course about which the department had concerns did just as well or better than students coming from the department's preferred course. This information was shared with the appropriate administrators, the department, and counselors. The study will be repeated next year, to determine how the department can best address students' needs through the use of these courses.

Another specific project was initially funded by a state-supported grant for instructional improvement. Given the desire to track the progress of remedial and limited-English-speaking students through the necessary English classes, a computer program was created to identify students who were beginning at the lowest level of English as a Second Language or remedial English. Their progress was monitored over six semesters, to see how many went on to complete higher levels. These are important outcome data for evaluating the effectiveness of instructional programs, as well as for ensuring access to the full range of courses for all students.

This study was conducted by a member of the research committee, with input from the campus researcher and assistance from the staff in computing services. Findings were initially shared with the committee, and now the study has become ongoing, with new data generated and analyzed each semester by the campus researcher and the interested committee member. Results will be shared each semester with the appropriate department and dean. The original findings indicated a large dropout rate among students in the first-level English class. This information, in large part, led to a major revision of the curriculum in the course.

Advantages and Disadvantages of the Model

As in other programs, the personalities and skills of the major participants play an important role in the success of the research program. It is important to build a model that does not rely on a particular individual or group to be effective, but rather centers on individuals who have the necessary skills and are interested in participating. The initial implementation of a model requires ongoing evaluation and feedback from participants and intended beneficiaries of research. The centralized-decentralized research model has been in operation at Allan Hancock College for less than one year and is still in the process of being evaluated and modified.

There are a number of advantages to this approach. First, the committee connects the research function to the mainstream of the college. Often in institutional settings, research seems to take place in a vacuum, with little input from faculty or staff members. The committee is broad-based and representative of the major groups on campus, including student services and instruction.

This model also allows for priority setting on research projects and creation of reasonable timelines. Since progress is reviewed regularly by the committee, bottlenecks and procedural problems are usually averted or resolved in an expedient manner.

Broad participation and support from administrators and faculty are possible because of their representation on the committee. The link with staff development, through funding of independent research grants, further fosters this support and involvement. The policy of wide dissemination helps to ensure that research results are tied to policy and decision making. The model is particularly sensible for smaller colleges because release time can be provided for qualified faculty members, and so the committee can be composed of knowledgeable staff in existing positions. This allows flexibility in regard to the initial investment required by the college and makes a research function possible without the expense of full-time staff.

The advantages are not limited to the committee. While the committee provides an excellent flow of information, in most instances it is not responsible for actually conducting the research. Having a part- or full-time researcher in addition to the committee is essential in getting the work done without placing unreasonable expectations on committee members, who already have full-time jobs. Committee members' willingness to serve depends on the fact that they are primarily guiding the process, rather than conducting the research. A campus can implement the model with a part-time researcher and then evaluate the need for a full-time position.

The disadvantage of the model is that it involves yet another committee, which requires representation from several campus groups. The committee must be a working body, willing to meet regularly and do its homework before meetings. Moreover, the relationship of the campus researcher to the committee is a delicate one; roles must be clear and complementary, rather than competitive. It would be easy for the campus researcher to interpret the committee's guidance as interference or criticism, and the committee could conceivably exceed its authority over the researcher's work. This is a sensitive balance, which relies on good communication among the parties. As in any other institutional process, time becomes the test of relative success. The model will continue to undergo evaluation and modification through experience with its products.

Marylin Orton is associate dean of student support services at Allan Hancock College, Santa Maria, California.

*The Kansas Community College Research Consortium was
organized to respond to increased demands for accountability
that were being made by the Kansas legislature and by local
governing boards.*

Research by Voluntary Consortium

Don Doucette, Jeffrey A. Seybert

While community colleges have historically organized consortia to undertake collaborative action for numerous and varied purposes, they have less
frequently organized into voluntary consortia for the purpose of conducting
institutional research. This chapter describes a consortium organized specifically and exclusively to conduct such research for community colleges
in Kansas. Its motivations for organizing, its operating procedures, and the
strengths and weaknesses of the studies conducted under its auspices are
generally representative of efforts that might be undertaken by similar
voluntary consortia organized for similar purposes. The Kansas Community
College Research Consortium (KCCRC) is not proposed as an ideal to be
imitated but rather as an example from which to learn.

Motivations for Organizing a Research Consortium

In fall 1983, an existing voluntary body, the Kansas Council of Community
College Presidents, commissioned two research studies: a study of the economic impact of the Kansas Community Colleges on their communities and
on the state, and a study of former students of the nineteen Kansas Community Colleges who subsequently transferred to the six public universities in
the state. The result of the presidents' action was the formation of the Kansas
Community College Research Consortium. The consortium ultimately conducted additional studies, including a reverse-transfer study and a longitudinal follow-up study of entering community college students, but it was the
commissioning of the first two studies that caused its formal establishment.

    The motivation among the presidents to form the consortium was the
shared need to respond to demands for accountability that were being increas-

ingly made by the Kansas legislature. To a lesser extent, the presidents were also responding to the similar demand of local governing boards. Under pressure from common external constituents, the presidents of the nineteen colleges commissioned research that they believed would demonstrate not only the value that their institutions had for the economies of their communities and the state but also the effectiveness with which their colleges performed a highly visible, traditional function—the transfer mission.

An underlying but equally compelling motivation for establishing a voluntary consortium to conduct research was that the majority of participating colleges were inadequately staffed to conduct these studies on their own. In 1983, only two of the nineteen colleges were staffed with professionals whose specific responsibility was institutional research. Some of the colleges used staff with principal responsibilities in other areas of the colleges (such as admissions and records, financial aid, and the business office) to conduct basic institutional research. Other colleges conducted little or no research other than that required to complete state-mandated reports. Thus, a consortium approach was used to compensate for the inadequate research resources of the individual colleges.

Finally, the studies in question were of the kind that require interinstitutional cooperation to achieve comprehensive results. The presidents understood that documenting the economic impact of all the community colleges in Kansas was more meaningful than conducting separate studies of the impact of individual colleges. Similarly, the performance of the entire system of community colleges in providing transfer students to the state's public universities was of specific interest to the state legislature. Since such studies had not previously been conducted in Kansas, it must also have appeared safer to the presidents to be entering uncharted waters—research on the impact and effectiveness of the colleges—as a group of nineteen institutions. Given the expressed enthusiasm of the presidents for the project, it would have been difficult for any individual president to decline to participate in a project so strongly supported by the majority of his or her peers. The motivation of the Kansas presidents to make efficient use of limited resources in responding to common demands for accountability was the most common reason for such a volunteer effort.

Description of the Model

Organization of the KCCRC. The presidents commissioned the community college that had the most comprehensive institutional research office in the consortium to coordinate the two studies and committed the other eighteen colleges to participate. Johnson County Community College (JCCC) agreed to assume the principal responsibility for conducting the studies and coordinating consortium efforts. Each of the participating colleges contributed $1,000 to support the studies, and each named a principal contact to coordinate its participation.

This organizational model reflected the reality of the Kansas Community Colleges when the consortium was formed: essentially, only one college was adequately staffed to coordinate the studies for all the colleges in the state. Since this college was willing to take the leadership role in what its president viewed as an important task, centralizing the responsibility for conducting the studies was seen as the most efficient approach available. The other eighteen colleges acted in a reviewing and advisory capacity, to ensure that the research design, procedures, and results reflected their interests and that the data were collected at their colleges in a coordinated fashion.

Each participating college involved various staff positions in the research efforts. Since only one institution other than JCCC had a full-time staff person conducting institutional research, participating colleges commandeered staff to assist, even though their primary responsibilities were in admissions and records, instruction and institutional development, student services, and the president's office. Some institutions shifted the responsibility for participating to different individuals in the college; for instance, a vice-president for business services assisted with the economic-impact study, but the same college's registrar was the key contact for the transfer study.

In all cases, participation was assigned to college staff in addition to their other responsibilities. While release time would have been preferable, it was not possible in most cases. The burden of participation became a point of contention and sometimes caused delays in completing tasks. Nevertheless, the fact that the presidents of the colleges maintained an interest in the consortium's efforts ensured the full participation and cooperation of the various staff members assigned to the projects. In no case was it actually necessary for the coordinator to threaten a call to the president to spur anyone's participation, but the availability of that option was well recognized by all involved.

Operating Procedures. Operating procedures, developed to meet the specific requirements of each of the studies, varied somewhat because of the different requirements of the studies. In general terms, the procedures followed by a consortium to conduct research are the same as those that would be followed in any other research. Nevertheless, the involvement of numerous parties and multiple institutions in voluntary efforts requires considerable attention to the process of conducting research, as well as considerable flexibility with regard to responsibilities and procedures. The following section describes how research objectives were determined, procedures carried out, projects monitored, results determined and disseminated, and institutional impacts identified in this series of studies.

Operating the Voluntary Consortium in Kansas

How Were Research Objectives Determined? In this case, the objectives of the two research studies initially commissioned by the Kansas Community College presidents were determined by the group as a whole. As previously mentioned, the presidents were motivated by calls for accountability from external constituents (chiefly the state legislature) and their local boards, and they collectively chose to pursue a research agenda to demonstrate the economic value of their colleges and the effectiveness of their colleges in performing the transfer function. Their setting of the research agenda reflected political realities, and their presumption was that the results of the studies would portray their colleges in a positive light.

Translating this broad research agenda into manageable research projects was left to the coordinator of the consortium, in consultation with participants from the various colleges involved in the studies. For each of the two studies, the coordinator drafted research plans that carefully detailed the research questions involved in the objectives articulated by the presidents. For instance, in the case of the transfer study, the question of how well community colleges were performing the transfer function was analyzed to include questions related to the number of Kansas community college transfers, transfer students' satisfaction with the community colleges, and the academic performance and progress of community college transfer students in comparison with students who began their studies at the universities.

After completion of the first two studies, the coordinator, on behalf of the participating researchers, prepared recommendations for future research for the presidents' council. The presidents approved subsequent proposals to continue the transfer study, to undertake a reverse-transfer study, and to initiate a long-term follow-up study of students. Once again, after the presidents had set the research agenda, the coordinator drafted plans to operationalize the broad research objectives and worked with participants in the consortium to develop specific research specifications.

How Were Procedures and Responsibilities Determined? Procedures and responsibilities were articulated in lengthy research specifications drafted by the coordinator for each study. These specifications detailed definitions, data elements, analytical procedures, reporting specifications, timelines, and responsibilities for all aspects of the studies. Draft specifications were sent to all participants for review and comment. In the case of the economic-impact study, which followed a published model, the specifications were essentially accepted as written. In the case of the transfer study, the coordinator met with the researchers from the state universities several times, to achieve consensus on definitions and procedures.

Responsibilities fell naturally and logically to various participants. Johnson County Community College, as the coordinator of the studies, simply performed all the tasks that would be expected of a priɪ researcher. Participants from the various colleges and universities ‚--formed the tasks that only they could do, principally providing data from their colleges in agreed-upon formats.

How Were Research Projects Monitored? Each project was monitored and managed by the principal researcher and coordinator at JCCC. Most formal communications were by mail, with telephone follow-up to encourage compliance with timelines. Several times, problems with definitions or procedures were called to the attention of the coordinator, and modifications in the research specifications were made. Formal changes were in writing, although much more common was a steady stream of telephone conversations regarding questions in the methodology or problems in data sources.

The groups met several times on the transfer study, to check progress and compare the experiences of the participating colleges, but the economic-impact study was so straightforward that it required no meetings. Whenever possible, the coordinator took the opportunity to arrange a meeting of the consortium (at least once a semester) in conjunction with other statewide meetings, to encourage group cohesion and exert peer pressure for timely completion of tasks.

How Were Results and Implications Determined? For each of the studies, participating colleges collected information on their own campuses and provided it to the principal researcher for analysis. The results of the study were derived from analyses conducted on data collected from multiple colleges; only JCCC had access to raw data for all colleges. The principal researcher drafted a report identifying the results of each study and provided the draft to the participants for review, discussion, and possible revision. The economic-impact study occasioned little discussion, but interpretation of the results of the transfer study was the subject of lengthy deliberations.

For each study, the principal researcher drafted a final report that represented the consensus of all participating colleges. To a limited degree, the report of the results was negotiated, but the implications of the results were not necessarily subject to the same consensus. The implication of the economic-impact study—that colleges provide substantial economic return to their communities—was clear to all; some colleges also concluded that they needed to be more careful to do business with local vendors, to maximize that impact. Participants in the transfer study agreed on the study's results but did not necessarily agree on its implications. The study noted that students had some difficulty moving from community colleges to the state universities, and the implications of this finding were viewed differently by the representatives of the various institutions.

How Were Results Disseminated? The consortium model almost guaranteed widespread dissemination of the research results. After consensus on the results was reached, a final report for each study was published by

JCCC. Initial distribution was to the presidents who had commissioned the study and to all participants. Multiple copies were then provided for distribution to interested parties throughout the state.

The principal researcher made several presentations on the studies, including testimony, based on the results, before several state legislative committees. JCCC took the leadership role in disseminating and explaining results at the statewide level, although other consortium members also participated. The colleges and universities involved in the study determined how they would disseminate the findings on their own campuses.

How Did Results Influence Institutional Changes? Because the consortium was organized specifically and exclusively to conduct research, no coordinated effort was made to address issues raised by the results of the studies. This was especially true of the economic-impact study, which had few if any practical implications for participating colleges. The results of the transfer study, however, were disaggregated by institution, and each college or university was able to compare its own performance of the transfer function with that of peer institutions. Several indicated that the results had caused careful examination of selected institutional practices related to transfer students, and some made changes in their policies and procedures.

Strengths and Weaknesses of Consortium Research

The strengths and weaknesses of the voluntary consortium approach to research are inherent in the nature of the multicollege consortium; most will apply to any such consortium, whether or not it is organized and operated similarly to KCCRC.

Design and Definitions. The design of most research efforts can be improved by a broad-based, collaborative review process involving researchers with different perspectives and expertise. In nearly all the studies conducted in Kansas, the research designs drafted by the coordinating institution were improved in the review process. Unexpected problems with definitions and procedures were corrected, ambiguous survey items were clarified, and unexamined assumptions were pointed out.

In research that involved multiple institutions, design and definitions were reduced to the lowest common denominator necessary to allow each institution to participate. The cohort analysis of the initial transfer study was specifically designed to accommodate the varying characteristics and levels of sophistication of the six state universities' student information systems. Nevertheless, only two could complete the analysis; in fact, those two institutions actually went beyond the common design specifications and conducted more elegant analyses, to answer questions of specific interest to them. The continuation of the transfer study demonstrated this critical weakness of consortium research by requiring the design of the cohort analysis to be modified, so that the study could be carried out through painstaking manual analysis of hard-copy student records; and even this lowest-common-denominator design could be used by only five of the universities.

Definitions also suffered from oversimplification, to accommodate the various ways in which different institutions maintain student records. One of the principal limitations of the transfer study was the simplistic definition of *community college transfer students* that was necessitated by multi-institutional participation. The only definition that the data bases of the six institutions could accommodate was "students enrolled in a state university who listed a Kansas community college as the 'institution last attended.' " Thus, the study had to treat every student equally who had reported a Kansas community college as the last institution attended, including the student who may have attended only a single course as a high school student, summer-session student, or part-time evening student and the student with two years of full-time community college experience. Moreover, the definition excluded students who may have had considerable community college experience but also intervening experiences at other institutions. No definition that included credit hours earned at or transferred from a Kansas community college, year of high school graduation, or attendance at multiple institutions could be accommodated by all the universities whose data were required for the study. In fact, the term *transfer student* was used sparingly in the report and was specifically excluded from its title because the consensus of the research group was that *transfer student* implied an orderly and traditional pattern of college and university attendance, which could not be assumed for all students covered by the study.

Perhaps even more dramatic was the failure of the study of reverse-transfer students, because of the inability of nineteen community colleges to develop and consistently implement a definition that adequately identified these students; their record systems simply varied too much in sophistication and thoroughness. In sharp contrast, however, was the relative ease and success of the joint study of the economic impact of the nineteen Kansas Community Colleges. Definitional problems for the numerous financial data that were required could easily have scuttled the study, but the chief business officers had developed a uniform chart of accounts, which not only ensured comparable data among the institutions but also simplified the design and execution of the study.

Leadership and Expertise. One of the principal motivations for engaging in consortium research efforts is to share resources, particularly research expertise, among a group of institutions. It is common, especially among community colleges, to find that there simply are not enough resources available to conduct all the research that either is requested or simply should be done to improve practice or respond to demands for accountability. The studies that were conducted by the Kansas consortium would not even have been attempted by the majority of the colleges without the assistance of shared expertise and resources.

Yet consortium research requires appropriate leadership. In the case of KCCRC, Johnson County Community College assumed the role of principal researcher and coordinator of research efforts. This role could not have been assumed effectively without the explicit support of the community college presidents (in this case, support was facilitated by the lack of alternatives). Nevertheless, such leadership is difficult to assert and awkward to exert. Even though JCCC was commissioned by the presidents to coordinate the studies, it was always in the position of having to obtain compliance from individuals over whom it exerted no real authority and little real influence. Threatening to go directly to the president of a college to ensure completion of a task by a deadline was always an option, but use of such force would have made future cooperation even more tentative. The trick in these efforts was not only to complete the study successfully but also to make everyone involved feel good about results and participation.

The role that JCCC played with the university researchers was quite different. Again, JCCC had the explicit support of the chief academic officers of the universities, but the participation of the researchers always depended on a collegial, voluntary relationship among professionals, generally senior to the principal researcher.

Consensus and Impact. Although the idea of negotiating the meaning of the results of a large-scale study may seem unacceptable to a professional researcher, such negotiations are a fact of life in consortium research. No results are value-free, and institutions are justifiably wary of invidious comparisons that will invariably be made and inappropriate conclusions that will invariably be drawn by those who insist on taking results out of context to demonstrate the validity of their own predetermined conclusions. Nevertheless, it is precisely this struggle, to reach consensus on the meaning of the research results and to agree on a final report, that increases the importance and impact of consortium research.

Once endorsed by a broad base of participants, research results are often largely immune to challenges and questions of validity, representativeness, and comprehensiveness that often plague studies conducted by single institutions. Studies conducted by a consortium are at least implicitly accepted by all members of the consortium, while those conducted by external third parties may be easier to dispute and ignore.

In the case of the Kansas consortium, the results of each study were accepted at face value, in large part because of the perception that they accurately and fairly represented all the public institutions in the state. The state legislature reviewed the results of particular interest and accepted them in place of a planned audit of the articulation process between community colleges and universities, which was to have been conducted by its own legislative research division. The chief academic officers of the universities recommended some changes in policies and procedures after reviewing the findings. Community college presidents, the initiators of the consortium effort, used the results to promote their cause, with the universities as well as with the state legislature. It is arguable that the same studies could not have received equal attention or had the same impact if they had been conducted in any other way.

Two Illustrative Studies

A total of five distinct studies were carried out by the Kansas Community College Research Consortium, of which the first two exemplify KCCRC's typical operating procedures.

Economic Impact Study. The more straightforward of these two studies was the first completed. After accepting responsibility for coordinating the study, the Office of Institutional Research at Johnson County Community College reviewed the various models for determining the economic impact of institutions of higher education and settled on a simplified model for community colleges, one developed by Ryan (1983) for New Jersey.

Design. JCCC adapted the model for the Kansas Community Colleges, developed an instrument and definitions to collect comparable data from each of the colleges, forwarded this information to the identified contact at each college for review, and then collected the required data. In this case, the review function performed by the individuals designated to coordinate their colleges' participation was perfunctory. In nearly all cases, the individuals so designated worked in the business offices and were the best individuals to collect the necessary data for their colleges but did not necessarily have research expertise or familiarity with the various models for conducting economic-impact studies.

Data Collection. With some prompting and considerable counseling about the most appropriate information to use in the study, each of the colleges provided all the necessary data. The process was greatly facilitated by the fact that the Kansas Community Colleges' chief business officers had recently adopted a uniform chart of accounts and, even more important, the presidents maintained an active interest in the progress of the study.

Analysis. JCCC collected data from the eighteen other community colleges and worked directly with a number of departments in Kansas state government to obtain the additional data required by the Ryan model. JCCC conducted the necessary analyses and prepared a draft report of the findings.

Reporting. Given the nature of economic-impact studies (the results of which depend more on the assumptions used in the study than on the precision of the data collected) and the high interest of the presidents who commissioned the study, the preliminary report was shared not only with the individuals participating in the study at each college but also with their presidents. Although the group conducting the study had never met, either to design the study or to collaborate on its methodology, the presidents met to discuss the report, as presented by the principal researcher. The presidents' review was nontechnical, and most of the discussion concerning the results focused on the conservative estimates used by the researcher. After this review, JCCC prepared and published a final report, which was broadly distributed and used in various political forums throughout the state. The results of the study—which demonstrated a very large and positive impact of the Kansas Community Colleges on their communities and on the state, as well as a large economic return for each tax dollar invested—were all the more credible because they were the results of a consortium effort that could boast 100 percent participation. One of the most enduring results of this first study was that the presidents' strong positive reception of the report provided impetus and support for additional research using the consortium model.

Community College Transfer Study. Although commissioned by the Kansas Council of Community College Presidents at the same time as the economic-impact study, the study of students moving from the Kansas Community Colleges to the state's public universities was considerably more complex. It required different operating procedures and more time to complete. The principal complexity was that the study could be conducted only in concert with two additional councils of representatives from the state universities, on which the study depended for data collection. In the absence of any state or official mandate, the sponsorship of the council of presidents was an important factor in persuading the Council of Chief Academic Officers of the universities to authorize the participation of the Council of Institutional Research Officers in a comprehensive statewide study of student mobility. Thus, the study became the project of two voluntary consortia representing twenty-five institutions.

Design. Johnson County Community College again assumed leadership in designing and coordinating the transfer study. Its Office of Institutional Research reviewed dozens of similar transfer studies conducted in other states and developed a three-part research design to study the number and characteristics of students moving from the Kansas Community Colleges to state universities, perceptions of these students at both types of institutions, and the academic performance, persistence, and degree achievement of matched cohorts of community college transfers and native university students.

The principal collaborative efforts were those between JCCC, which represented the consortium of community colleges, and the institutional researchers from the state universities. After several meetings characterized by negotiations concerning appropriate definitions, legitimate survey questions, and fair comparisons, research specifications were developed, to be implemented primarily by JCCC and the six state universities.

Data Collection. The nature of the study required researchers at the state universities to play the principal role in collecting the data on which the rest of the study depended. The three-part study required three different types of data. Using the negotiated research specifications, each of the six universities attempted to provide comparable data for each part. All six were able to identify all transfer students (including a sample of students to be surveyed) according to the agreed-upon definition. Only two of the six universities, however, were able to complete the rather complex programming required to construct selected student cohorts retrospectively and to follow them through several subsequent semesters.

JCCC developed the survey instrument, which was reviewed and approved by all community colleges and universities participating in the cooperative study. JCCC mailed the survey, using labels supplied by the six universities, and then conducted routine follow-up procedures and collected the completed surveys.

Analysis. To provide the data required by the research specifications, each of the universities developed computer programs to run against their historical student records. The results represented a first stage of analysis. Since all six universities used somewhat different records systems, however, each with different anomalies, the results from the universities needed to be combined appropriately and analyzed as a whole to answer the questions posed by the study.

JCCC coordinated this final analysis of data from several sources, including survey data returned directly to the college. While analysis of the survey data was easily computerized, the summary data provided in hard copy by each university needed to be combined manually so that results could be interpreted for the entire state. Each university provided summary data, not access to the individual records of which the data were composed. Thus, these data could not be disaggregated and combined with results from the other five universities but needed to be treated as they were, which required numerous explanatory footnotes.

Reporting. A report detailing the results of the study was drafted by JCCC for review by all participating institutions. Although this particular study required the active participation of only the six universities and JCCC (as the representative of the community colleges in the state), all twenty-five state institutions were asked to review the report because it contained data on transfer students either from or enrolled at all or most of them. The presidents of the community colleges were sent the report for review, and they either reviewed it themselves or passed it on to more appropriate individuals. Review by the universities was coordinated through the principal research contacts who had participated in the study.

The most sensitive issue that emerged from these reviews was disaggregation of results for each institution. As could have been predicted, institutions that felt that the report would provide the opportunity for invidious comparisons were concerned about disaggregation. Others argued that identification of the community colleges that transfer students came from and of the universities where they enrolled was critical. A compromise solution was reached on how the data were reported. Specifically, results concerned with the number and characteristics of transfer students were disaggregated to identify sending and receiving institutions. Because the number of students ranged from 6,000 in the first year of the study to over 10,000 in the fourth and final year, disaggregation was practical and provided meaningful displays of data. Survey results concerned with the more sensitive issues of student satisfaction were combined, as were the results of the comparative academic performance, persistence, and degree achievement of cohorts of community college transfers and native university students.

Interpretation of the results was carefully scrutinized, especially by the participating researchers at the universities, who were well attuned to the subtleties of the data and sensitive to the implications of some results. The final report negotiated among the researchers did not compromise the integrity of the results in any way, but it contained very careful and muted conclusions, with numerous qualifications and explanatory footnotes. The first conclusion in the executive summary of the report was said to be "subject to qualifications due to limitations in the data," and the summary concluded with the following statement: "The substantial limitations of the data which constitute the findings of the study and the paradoxical nature of some of the results are discussed at some length in the report. These strongly suggest both that the findings need to be qualified and that future research needs to be conducted." The preface to the report also warned the reader to avoid all interinstitutional comparisons as likely to be misleading.

Consequently, unlike the short, nontechnical report of the economic-impact study, the report on the transfer phenomenon in Kansas was lengthy and complex and depended on summary sections, color coding, and oral presentation of results. The principal researcher from JCCC made presentations of the study results, first for the community college presidents and then for various constituencies throughout the state. These included two joint presentations with a representative of the university research consortium before committees of the state legislature.

Because of widespread participation, the care with which a consensus report was negotiated, and high interest in the subject, the study received considerable attention from important constituencies including the presidents of the community colleges, the presidents of the universities, and the state legislature. Moreover, because the report documented substantial growth in the number of transfer students, as well as their generally positive experiences and some reasonably discrete problem areas, it provided a useful basis for improving institutional practices.

Conclusion

There are appropriate motivations for forming voluntary consortia to conduct institutional research. Among these are the need to share limited resources and use them effectively, the usefulness of a group of community colleges' common response to demands for accountability from the same external constituencies, and the appropriateness of certain kinds of studies for consortium-based research efforts. In fact, statewide studies involving numerous institutions among which students move rather freely are particularly well suited to research by consortia.

There are limitations inherent in the conduct of consortium research. These are chiefly associated with the accommodations in definitions, design, and procedures that need to be made so that all members of a group can participate. There are also complicated issues of leadership, control, and influence. In certain circumstances, however, the results of research studies conducted and endorsed by consortia have the greatest possible impact and influence.

Reference

Ryan, G. J. *Handbook for Conducting a Study of the Economic Impact of a Community College.* Lincroft, N.J.: Brookdale Community College, 1983.

Don Doucette is associate director of the League for Innovation in the Community College, Laguna Hills, California, and was director of research, evaluation, and instructional development at Johnson County Community College, Kansas, when the consortium described in this chapter was initiated and these studies were conducted.

Jeffrey A. Seybert is director of research, evaluation, and instructional development at Johnson County Community College, Kansas.

States and colleges can cooperate to develop and conduct institutional research. When certain prerequisites are in place, this model can lift the effectiveness of research across the whole state.

t-Test for Two: A State-Local Research Partnership

Daniel D. McConochie, James D. Tschechtelin

One of the most dominant characteristics of community college systems in most states is variance among the colleges. Within a single state, there may be large colleges with extensive institutional research conducted by a large staff, as well as small colleges with little institutional research and no full-time staff. What approach provides an effective statewide research program, promotes research at small colleges, and does not intrude on the research of the large colleges? One answer is a state-local institutional research partnership, and this chapter describes such a model (see Table 1). The partnership seeks to meet the research needs of the Maryland State Board for Community Colleges and the individual colleges in a way that minimizes duplication of effort and accomplishes projects that could not be initiated with the data or the monetary and human resources of only one college.

Overview of Maryland Community Colleges

Maryland's community college system encompasses seventeen community colleges, ranging from a small college (600 credit students) serving rural, small-town communities to a large multicampus college serving 22,000 students at suburban and urban centers. Each college is governed by its own board of trustees and is supported by a financing system that provides state funds, county support for community colleges, and tuition.

The state board for community colleges is responsible for coordination, policy analyses, and reporting to the legislature, to the executive branch of state government, and to federal agencies. Over the years, it has also acquired the role of reporting data trends and intercollege comparisons

Table 1. Process for State-Local Research Partnership

Task	State	State-Local Partnership	Local
Define research needs		XX	
Design study and instruments		XX	
Print instruments	XX		
Mail instruments			XX
Enter data and produce computer analysis	XX		
Write and report recommendations		XX	XX
Disseminate report	XX		XX
Act on recommendations	XX		XX

to the colleges, for internal management. The board's eight professional staff members work directly with each college and with strong statewide organizations of college professionals. These groups—representing presidents, finance directors, directors of facilities, continuing education deans, instructional deans, directors of computer centers, and institutional research directors—form a critical part of our model of cooperative research.

Description of the Model

The Maryland Community College Research Group (MCCRG), like similar statewide community college groups, has a representative from each of the seventeen community colleges, is chaired by a college research director, and meets regularly. While relationships among the colleges, the MCCRG, and the state board are the primary concern of this chapter, the other professional groups are often involved in determination of research issues, discussion of objectives, and dissemination of research results. For instance, when state law required each college to identify out-of-state peer colleges, the finance directors' group, meeting with the state board's director of finance, discussed alternative strategies, examined methods for collecting data, and formulated a list of research questions. Similarly, the statewide group representing the directors of facilities identified issues involving state and local criteria for space allocation and designed research objectives and data-collection efforts to address the need for further information concerning current and projected space utilization.

Often, an issue will be of concern to more than one of these groups, and task subcommittees are appointed by the chair of the two groups to meet with the state board staff, conduct research, and report to the larger groups. For example, recent concerns with graduation and retention rates generated interest among instructional deans and institutional researchers, and a joint subcommittee has begun examining alternative definitions, data sources, and methods of analysis for this sensitive issue.

Because the statewide groups meet regularly and work closely with the state board's staff, many research projects can be handled by such subcommittees. Other projects, because of their recurring nature, have become institutionalized—some because of the recurring need for particular information at the state level, and some because the information is needed at the campus level.

Research projects conducted with this model have included the following:

- Regular follow-up surveys of graduates, conducted since 1972
- Cohort studies, which follow entering students through two- and four-year tracking systems
- Analyses of transfer students' patterns and success
- Surveys of the employers of graduates
- Examination of the outcomes of continuing education courses
- Analyses of costs per full-time-equivalent (FTE) student in disciplines at each college, and comparison of these costs and FTE trends at peer colleges
- Cooperative development of records systems, with common data-element definitions.

How Are Research Objectives Determined?

When a research project is unique to a community college, the institutional research director, the president, and the college's board of trustees decide research objectives and resource priorities. Often, the results of such a project will be shared at an MCCRG meeting, and the project will be conducted by other colleges or picked up as a statewide project by the group and the state board. Individual colleges first conducted economic-impact studies and, by sharing their results, convinced others of the value of conducting local studies, as well as a statewide economic-impact study of the community colleges (Linthicum, 1978, 1986). Other research projects, while seen as valuable by particular colleges, have never become statewide projects.

Projects that have generated cooperation and collaboration among all the colleges have generally arisen from local research interests that were affecting a number of the colleges, or from state information requirements generated by the legislature, the Maryland Higher Education Commission, or groups such as the state board's Committee on the Future of Maryland Community Colleges. For example, a number of colleges may express local concerns regarding demographic changes related to population mobility, aging of the county's population, age of their faculty, or the enrollment and success of students in a particular program area. In most cases, for such a topic to become the subject of a statewide project, there would need to be a consensus (or strong core of support) within the MCCRG that this was an important topic, which would benefit from a comparative perspective. For example, are the faculty at one college unique, or are all the community college faculty in the state going to retire in 1998? There would also be a discussion and a consensus in the Maryland Council of Community College Presidents on the broad research goals. The research design would generally be the work of the MCCRG. Plans and procedures for data collection and analysis would be shared and agreed to, and the statewide study would be conducted.

When research projects are generated from legislative inquiries, statutory requirements, or from other statewide groups, a similar process is followed. The presidents' group is briefed on the broad information request. The MCCRG then becomes involved in the design of the data-gathering instruments and in decisions on whether currently collected data could be used to answer some of the inquiries.

Procedures and Responsibilities

Over the years, as more research projects have been conducted on a statewide basis, procedures and responsibilities have been shared in a number of ways, in response to particular research needs, funding sources, resource demands, and available human resources. Currently, when a new project is being developed, there will be unique project features, but there will also be a pattern of successful procedures identified from past experiences. The pattern used in the annual follow-up studies (conducted as a statewide project since 1972) is fairly typical and usually serves as the model when procedures for new projects are being developed.

Application of the Model

In the case of the follow-up studies, the MCCRG decides on the research goals and the design of the instruments. Subcommittees or individual members may be assigned the tasks of reviewing the usefulness of old questions and reviewing the need for new questions. The surveys used in prior studies are examined by the group, to ensure continuity for trend analysis, to add new questions for assessing current interests, and to drop items that are no longer of interest.

The state board coordinates the development of the research instrument and pays for the printing of the survey. Each college is responsible for providing mailing labels, and all conduct the field administration of the survey. The survey is mailed along with a cover letter from the college president, and surveys are returned to the college. If questions arise, the respondent is encouraged to call a contact person in the institutional research office. The state board reimburses the colleges for some costs.

Data about each student in the study population are provided to the state board by the individual colleges. These data include demographic characteristics, goals from when the student first entered the college, and such other data as grade point average, highest degree, and credit hours earned. The state board enters the survey data into a computer file and merges it with the data provided by the colleges. The state board analyzes the data and provides two printouts to each college: an early-edit run that the college must review and correct, if necessary, and a second run that allows the college to compare its students and survey respondents with those at peer colleges and in the state system as a whole.

Each college, at this point, becomes responsible for writing a report using its own data, the data from its peer colleges, and the statewide results; comparisons with the results from other individually identified colleges are not provided by the state board. Each college is also responsible for the local dissemination of its results and for the use of these results in evaluation of college services and in strategic planning, as well as in such forums as faculty workshops, where survey results are discussed further.

The state board's staff often helps review prepublication reports but generally takes no active role in the reporting of a college's results. The state board writes a report or a series of reports using the statewide results. Statewide reports are generally shared with the college research offices for review and comment before publication. Data from the survey are combined with data on enrollment, degrees, manpower projections, and costs in the state board's data-monitoring system, which monitors each instructional program in the state. The survey data, used with trend data from previous surveys and other data sources, may be analyzed to examine current policy issues (such as nursing education, financial aid policies, and regional manpower patterns) that have become statewide or legislative issues.

How Are Research Projects Monitored?

Timetables for projects are established by the MCCRG as part of research design and procedures. State board staff remind individual colleges of deadlines and occasionally exert pressure on a college that has fallen behind in its part of a project. Data quality and integrity are primarily the responsibility of the college research office. The monthly agenda of the MCCRG meetings includes a review of the progress of the current research projects and an opportunity for colleges to share reports with others working on similar reports. When a state report breaks new ground (for example, the recent reports on the outcomes of continuing education), the report is presented to and discussed by the Maryland Council of Community College Presidents before dissemination of the research results.

Identifying Results and Implications

The state board staff generally drafts a report or a technical memo that includes recommendations for action and draws implications. These drafts are reviewed by the MCCRG and other groups in the community college system. Consensus is sought on the meaning of the data or on the perception that the data at least support the implications and recommendations in the draft report. Data and reports that deal with transfer to the four-year college system in Maryland are reviewed with appropriate individuals in that system.

In the state board's data-monitoring system there are "flags" that note when the data from a program are significantly different from the results for other programs at the college or are different from similar programs at other colleges. For example, a program is flagged for additional review when the percentage of its graduates working full-time in a related job is widely divergent from the statewide result for similar programs. These "flags" have been reviewed and agreed on by the instructional deans. A state board recommendation will often be reexamined at the campus level, to see if campus data support the recommendation. Likewise, a campus report may draw attention to aspects of the data that will then be examined at the statewide level. In recent years, for example, a campus report on the characteristics and success of graduates of a data-processing program prompted statewide review of the follow-up results of this program. The state review in turn prompted other campuses to examine the program.

How Are Results Disseminated?

The periodic follow-up studies of students are representative of how results from the state-local partnership projects are used and disseminated at the local and state levels. The recent follow-up study of continuing education students, the 1988 follow-up of students who first entered the colleges in 1984, and other research studies (concerning such topics as transfer students' success) have followed similar patterns of dissemination. A statewide report is produced by the state board's staff, documenting methodology, response rate, major findings, and implications. Most colleges produce similar reports, using their campus data, and compare these data with prior study results and with results from peer colleges, as well as with statewide results. The research results also are included in the ongoing program evaluation of the state board's data-monitoring system. Administrators and faculty of individual programs are responsible for reviewing and drawing implications from results for their particular programs.

At the state level, the research is summarized for discussion at the president's council and for inclusion in the state board's newsletter, which is sent to faculty and staff at each campus. Graphs and articles are used to draw attention to particular issues (examples of these efforts have been special reports on transfer education and nursing programs). Executive summaries and graphs are prepared to present the results to legislators and budget analysts at legislative hearings and at interagency meetings. Results are presented to special-interest groups (such as the state Council on Vocational Education and the Maryland Higher Education Commission) and to statewide groups from the community college campuses (such as administrators of developmental education programs). The data-monitoring system has led to the elimination of one hundred credit occupational programs during the past ten years. This accomplishment has been important in justifying requests for increased state aid to Maryland community colleges. At the campus level, the institutional research director provides similar summaries and makes presentations to the deans of the college, faculty workshops, community groups, the college boards of trustees, and sometimes county budget hearings.

Determining Changes

The state board uses research data for policy analysis, program evaluation, and review of new program proposals. Poor job-placement rates in human services programs led to a statewide evaluation of those programs and to elimination of several. Knowledge of the characteristics and goals of nursing students and follow-up information on job location and starting salaries were used in examining proposed state-funded financial aid for nurses. Research results were also used in deciding whether a new nursing program was needed in one region of the state.

At the community college campus, data from campus and statewide research projects are used by administrators, faculty, and local boards of trustees when institutional changes are considered. Data from a particular campus, indicating that some students may be unhappy with their preparation for transfer or have lost credits when they tried to transfer, may initiate a college review of the situation surrounding the transfer of these students, a review of the curriculum, and other actions by the college. In one case, a president decided to change the college's promotional strategy to emphasize positive data about student outcomes in the college viewbook. In another case, a president decided to use statewide data to set a strategic objective for the college to rank in the top third among Maryland community colleges on several key outcome variables.

Strengths of the State-Local Model

The strengths of this model of collaborating on research projects lie in its ability to design and carry out projects that meet multiple needs. The mutual development of strong research designs permits meeting both campus and state needs for research information. Duplication of effort is avoided, but, more important, projects can be undertaken that would not be as feasible or useful if only one campus were involved. Involvement of the presidents' council and the instructional deans in identifying research needs, and the involvement of the MCCRG in the design, administration, and analysis of surveys, promotes institutional ownership of results and recommendations. The ability of a college to compare its results to those of peer colleges and to statewide results aids in the interpretation of data. The wide community of researchers involved with the same data base creates a variety of perspectives and expertise. Research reports are shared among colleges, and a researcher on one campus has a network of peers with similar data on research issues. The many resources of the state board permit even the smallest colleges to conduct fairly sophisticated and involved studies of credit students, transfer to four-year colleges, continuing education students, economic impacts, costs, and employers.

Weaknesses of the Model

The attention that must be given to coordination, and to careful planning of those projects that span all colleges, may prolong a project by several years. Communication and trust among all parties must be high. If the representative of one college is missing from a meeting, or if there is a personnel change in a college research office, there may be misunderstandings over why and when some element has been added or changed. For results to be useful in statewide analyses, and for one college to be able to compare itself with its peers, there must also be consistency in the quality of the data from all colleges. If, for example, in the report-writing stage of a study, the writer becomes aware that one college has misinterpreted a data element or miscoded categories of ethnicity, the consequences will affect all the data, not just the results for that particular college.

   In addition to the need for increased coordination, planning, and monitoring of data quality across institutions, there is the danger that the research design and questions will tend toward the lowest common denominator. Should the study accommodate colleges that have the fewest resources to commit? What happens when fifteen out of seventeen colleges can provide student-placement scores from their mainframe files, but the other two keep this information in file cabinets? Maryland studies have generally tended to push colleges to upgrade their data systems.

Case Study

The 1988 follow-up study of the 1984 entrants illustrates many of the features of this state-local research model. MCCRG, reacting to campus and state needs for information concerning student outcomes, developed a research design that included college-provided information on the goals and characteristics of students who first entered the colleges in fall 1984. College-provided data included such outcome measures as highest degree earned, grade point average, and credit hours earned. During the previous ten years, the definitions of these college-provided data elements had been agreed on by MCCRG and the Association of Data Processing Directors. Data on students' goals and reasons for attendance were available for the 1988 study because prior to 1984 there had been agreement among the colleges on the importance of collecting such data. The colleges had agreed on how to collect and store this information so that it would be available for subsequent studies.

The MCCRG then developed a survey, to be sent to these 1984 entrants in spring 1988. It included items dealing with the entrants' experiences at the college, their evaluations of services and instructional programs, and their status and activities since leaving the college. In most cases, responses to these items were seen as important, from both the state's and the colleges' perspectives. In other cases (such as the question "Did you use the job-placement service?"), the results were of primary interest at the college level. The survey instrument was drafted by the state board after statewide workshops and was reviewed and changed by MCCRG and other statewide groups.

The state board printed and distributed the questionnaire to the colleges. The colleges mailed the survey to all their 1984 entrants and mailed a second survey to nonrespondents. The returned surveys were sent to the state board, where they were entered into files and then matched and merged with the student records containing data on student characteristics, goals, and college outcomes. The state board staff used a statistical program to compare the characteristics of survey respondents and nonrespondents and to conduct a preliminary analysis of the data for each college file.

These results were sent to each college and reviewed by its survey administrator. After this review, the individual college files were combined into a master file, and each college received a customized analysis showing the results for that college, for a self-selected group of peer colleges (not individually identified campuses), and for the state in general. At the individual-college level, these data will be used in reports, faculty workshops, program and service evaluations, and presentations to the board of trustees. The data will also be useful as each college begins responding to a recent legislative mandate to develop a campus accountability plan and annual report. Smaller colleges without full-time institutional research positions now have data from a relatively sophisticated survey that can be used in the development of an accountability report or in an accreditation-related self-study.

Conclusion

State higher education and community college agencies are becoming more concerned about accountability and outcome measures. At the same time, many individual community colleges are increasingly interested in assessment. Both trends, the state and the local, are interrelated, and both need a solid foundation of institutional research. The Maryland model of state-local partnership for institutional research has served both levels well in the past decade. The state-local research partnership has saved money and energy while producing research that has made a difference in education.

With its state-local partnership, Maryland has developed data systems and applied them to numerous research studies, with many positive results. The model, however, requires mutual trust and an active statewide organization of institutional research directors who are committed to the state-local model. The model is not really complicated. It involves people talking together about mutual needs and goals and cooperating to meet them.

References

Linthicum, D. S. *The Economic Impacts of Maryland Community Colleges.* Annapolis: Maryland State Board for Community Colleges, 1978. (ED 158 804)

Linthicum, D. S. *Economic Development Through Education.* Annapolis: Maryland State Board for Community Colleges, 1986. (ED 259 803)

Daniel D. McConochie is director of planning and research at the Maryland State Board for Community Colleges.

James D. Tschechtelin is executive director of the Maryland State Board for Community Colleges.

*State mandates for research and accountability are met through a
collaborative approach between the state's higher education agency
and its colleges and universities.*

The State Agency–
College-Mandated Approach

Madan Capoor, Edward Morante

The purpose of this chapter is to describe two statewide assessment programs mandated by the state of New Jersey and how they offset the institutional research and evaluation agendas and activities at the college level.
Through this description, the state agency–college-mandated approach to
research will be illustrated. The statewide assessment programs described
are the Basic Skills Assessment Program (BSAP) and the College Outcomes
Evaluation Program (COEP). The state agency is the New Jersey Department
of Higher Education, and the colleges involved are all the state public
colleges and universities and some New Jersey private higher education
institutions.

Until only ten or fifteen years ago, the external assessment of higher
education institutions and programs was almost exclusively conducted by
regional or specialized accrediting agencies. State departments or coordinating boards exercised fiscal and program-approval control but were rarely
involved directly with the assessment of institutions or their programs.
Much has changed in the last ten years. Declines in SAT and ACT mean
scores, as well as the subsequent discovery that a large number of students
graduating from high schools were seriously deficient in basic skills, general
knowledge, and problem-solving skills, led to a number of critical reports on
the country's educational system. Skepticism regarding the effectiveness of
the educational process has in more recent years spread to higher education.
There have been rising demands for stricter measures of accountability.

Higher education leaders in New Jersey had the foresight to play a
leadership role in responding to these concerns, instead of waiting to
respond to legislative mandates or public outcry. After a report by a blue-

ribbon panel of higher education representatives, the state board of higher education created the statewide Basic Skills Assessment Program in 1977. The mandatory program was designed to assess the basic skills and proficiencies of entering college freshmen and evaluate the effectiveness of college remedial programs. Reports on the results of statewide testing and on assessments of the effectiveness of institutional remedial programs have been submitted annually to the board.

Data on the performance of remedial and nonremedial students have raised some questions about standards in courses at some colleges. In 1983, the statewide Task Force on Pre-College Preparation recommended raising both high school and college standards. Specifically, the task force recommended the creation of an eleventh-grade high school graduation test, as well as a test for college sophomores. Responding to this, and to a demand for greater accountability of institutions of higher education, in 1985 the board of higher education outlined the parameters of a statewide program for outcomes assessment and approved the implementation of the College Outcomes Evaluation Program.

The principal purposes of both BSAP and COEP are to improve the quality of information available for institutional accountability and to provide an impetus to institutions for improving the educational process and its outcomes. Unlike more traditional assessment and accreditation programs, both of these efforts focus on the direct assessment of students' learning. The state does not mandate priorities for institutional research; these are set by the institutions themselves. As basic skills and college outcomes are related to the core mission of a college, however, its institutional research and assessment activities are significantly affected by the demands of state assessment programs. Moreover, at institutions that did not have fully functional institutional research programs, the state programs have provided the impetus to develop and expand resources for conducting institutional research and assessment.

Description of the Model

Creating the Need: Statewide Assessment Programs. Under the Basic Skills Assessment Program, all public colleges in the state (plus eleven private colleges that have joined the program voluntarily) are required to test all incoming freshmen with the New Jersey College Basic Skills Placement Test (NJCBSPT), developed by the Basic Skills Council, an advisory group created by the board of higher education. The NJCBSPT consists of a reading-comprehension test, a sentence-sense test (which is an objective writing test), an essay, a computation test, and an elementary algebra test. Public colleges are also required to set minimum standards or placement criteria within specified limits in each of four skill areas. These provide the basis on which students are identified as needing remediation. Students identified as lacking adequate basic skills must be enrolled in appropriate remedial courses within a specified time and must pass those courses before attempting any related college courses. In addition, all colleges are required by the Basic Skills Council to submit comprehensive outcome data on the effectiveness of their remedial programs.

The Response: A State Agency–College-Mandated Approach. Virtually all the specifics of BSAP were not created by the state but are the result of a collaborative process, in which faculty and staff from colleges actively participated at every stage to shape the program. The design and operation of this collaborative process represent the state agency–college-mandated approach to research. The statewide Basic Skills Council, appointed after the 1977 decision of the board of higher education to create BSAP, is the entity that fulfills the objectives for which the model exists. The council consists of three representatives from Rutgers University, two from the state colleges, three from the community colleges, one from the New Jersey Institute of Technology, one from a private college, two from the public at large, two from the Department of Higher Education (DHE), and the director of BSAP as an ex officio member. The director of BSAP is a full-time DHE employee but until recently was on loan to DHE for two years from one of the state colleges.

How Research Objectives Are Determined

To develop the basic-skills program, the council appointed three subcommittees, consisting of faculty and staff from the colleges. Two committees, the Reading and Writing Committee and the Mathematics Committee, developed the relevant portions of the NJCBSPT and will create new forms of the test every year. A third committee, the Assessment Committee, developed a system for collecting data from the institutions, to permit a state-level assessment of the character and effectiveness of institutional remedial programs. The data requested from each public college include number and percent of students tested who are required to be tested, number and percent of students identified for remediation in each skill area, number and percent of remedial students who enrolled in the required remedial courses, number and percent of students who successfully completed the final level of remediation in each skill area, and results on the posttest (a different form of the placement test) taken after completing needed remediation in each skill area. In addition, data are reported on three comparison groups in each skill area, for full-time students only. These groups consist of those not needing remediation, those needing remediation and completing it, and those needing remediation but not completing it. These data include retention rates, passing rates in subsequent skill-related college-level courses, college-level credits attempted and earned, percent of students who achieved a grade point average (GPA) of 2.0 or higher in college-level courses, and successful survival rate (continuing in college with a GPA of 2.0 or above).

Procedures and Responsibilities

By following the state guidelines, which are revised and reissued every year by the Basic Skills Council, each public college prepares a report, including a description of remedial programs and data on the performance of students who begin at the college in a particular fall. Performance data are reported on remedial and nonremedial students for four semesters. Each institution is urged to conduct additional studies and data analyses, in order to develop more detailed and specific information for improving its programs.

Using the institutional reports, the Assessment Committee develops the statewide report by means of the following procedure. BSAP staff in the Department of Higher Education prepare data profiles for each institution in each skill area. These data profiles are sent to the respective institutions for review, correction, and amplification. Each member of the Assessment Committee is then assigned three or four colleges (other than his or her own) for preparing assessment reports. On the basis of institutional data profiles and background information provided in the text of the institutional reports, critical profiles of four skill programs (reading, writing, computation, and algebra) are prepared for each institution. In its most recent report, the Assessment Committee developed provisional standards on each outcome indicator and assessed institutional performance against these standards.

Both the Basic Skills Council and its Assessment Committee have from the beginning rejected the idea of comparing institutions on individual outcome indicators. It has been strongly and consistently maintained that, because of the nonexperimental design of the assessment model, no single outcome indicator can be meaningfully interpreted to assess the effectiveness of a remedial program. Hence, it has been considered essential that all the indicators for a program should be reviewed together and interpreted in conjunction with one another.

The profiles of institutional basic-skills programs prepared by members of the Assessment Committee are discussed by the full committee, revised, and resubmitted for review by the full committee. This process is repeated until the committee is satisfied with the reports. The criteria used in reviewing a report are that it should be objective and fair, emphasizing each program's strengths and weaknesses, and that uniformity of standards, terminology, and tone should be maintained. Institutional reports are then sent to the respective institutions for review and comment before they are submitted to the board of higher education and published. After the board accepts the reports, copies are sent to the institutions, which are requested to review them and correct any weaknesses in their programs. Over time, such reports are used to monitor improvement.

Two Examples

Basic Skills Assessment Program. Before 1976, Middlesex County College did not systematically test incoming students or provide any substantial remedial services. After creation of an office of institutional research, in 1976, an office of testing was set up. The Nelson-Denny Reading Test and the California Achievement Test in mathematics were used to test a sample of incoming students in fall 1977. It was not until the fall of 1979, however, a year after BSAP became operational, that a system was initiated for identifying remedial students on the basis of NJCBSPT results and placing them in appropriate remedial courses.

Because of the state mandate and the fact that 65 percent of incoming students need remedial help in one or more areas, the college and its Office of Research and Planning (ORP) are heavily involved with basic skills–related activities. ORP not only has to maintain and generate data and information necessary to respond to the state data requirements, it also has to undertake research and data analysis to satisfy internal demands for information needed for college decision making related to the basic-skills program. College-determined research questions may concern the effectiveness of placement criteria in correctly placing students in or excluding them from remedial courses; the appropriateness of the level of remedial courses; the appropriateness of exit criteria in remedial courses; which college-level courses students can or cannot take before completing their remediation; relative incidence and success of remediation among ethnic groups; relative effectiveness of computer-assisted instruction versus traditional classroom instruction; relative effectiveness of a two-course sequence given over two semesters versus over a single semester; and monitoring of the performance of remediated students in college-level courses, to determine the effectiveness of instruction and the appropriateness of the exit criteria in remedial courses.

To respond to such research issues, ORP creates a discrete longitudinal data file for every fall-entering cohort. This file includes high school and demographic background data (including responses to the freshman questionnaire), test scores, remedial placement, semester and grades for all remedial courses and for a selected number of key college-level courses, posttest scores, enrollment data for six semesters, credits attempted and earned, GPA, and so on. The file is updated every semester. Given the comprehensive nature of the data available on each fall-entering cohort, the basic-skills file is used not only to generate information related to basic skills but also to conduct other research studies, such as on retention and on early identification of potential dropouts.

College Outcomes Evaluation Program. COEP represents a second system for accountability and improvement of higher education in New Jersey. It is both ambitious and comprehensive in its attempt to assess institutional effectiveness. The approach taken with COEP was based on work with BSAP and balances local initiatives with centrally defined measures and indicators. For example, an advisory committee, and four subcommittees consisting of representatives from different institutions, labored for two years in developing program recommendations. A COEP council and four committees (again including faculty and staff from public and private colleges) are now engaged in developing a statewide test, analyzing students' performance data, and developing guidelines for institutional assessment in other areas. COEP has also hired several consultants, both to review COEP recommendations and to offer workshops for college representatives. COEP consists of seven components: general intellectual skills (GIS) assessment; institutional assessment (in terms of students' performance); assessment of general education; assessment in the major; assessment of students' satisfaction and personal development; outcomes of faculty research, scholarship, and creative expression; and assessment of community impact.

Only in the area of GIS will a common statewide test be used. This test is being cooperatively developed among state agency and college representatives, with technical assistance from the Educational Testing Service. Institutional assessment (in terms of students' performance) is the only other area in which common measures will be collected by the state. These data on performance include retention and graduation rates, grade point averages, and credits completed and are generated by means of a statewide records system. All the remaining areas are assessed with locally developed measures and procedures that follow general state guidelines. Thus, the requirement for statewide measures of institutional effectiveness has yielded significant interaction among college and state agency personnel and resulted in a process for exchanging ideas and procedures throughout the state.

Institutional Responses

Each public college in New Jersey was asked to appoint someone to coordinate COEP activities within the institution and act as a liaison to COEP. Many colleges have set up new committees or reassigned existing committees to address the COEP requirements. Middlesex County College decided to take a slightly different approach. It was decided that the primary focus of the college's effort in this area should be on identifying and making internal changes to improve the quality of education. The state requirements would be kept in mind and responded to in this larger context. In other words, instead of allowing the state demands to set the institutional agenda, the college would develop its own priorities and respond to the state requirements within those priorities.

The primary reason for establishing this procedure was that the college already had a well-established system for program assessment. As participants in the Cyclical Program Review Process (an experiment to try an alternate method of self-study in fulfilling the requirements for regional accreditation), all departments in the college, instructional as well as non-instructional, conduct comprehensive self-assessment on a five-year cycle. Each year a number of departments engage in self-study, and every year a visiting team (appointed by the Commission on Higher Education of the Middle States Association of Schools and Colleges) visits the college to review the departments according to approved assessment guidelines.

The college has completed four cycles of the program-review process and assessment procedures, including collection and analysis of program-based data. The college is obligated to accommodate and integrate any new state-mandated demands for assessment with its existing structures and procedures. Nevertheless, the college's program-review process does not yield data on some areas required by COEP; for example, the Cyclical Program Review Process has not attempted to deal directly with learning outcomes. Because COEP focuses largely on assessing learning outcomes, activities conducted in responding to COEP would be complementary to the college's past efforts in conducting program assessment.

In responding to increased demands for improvement in educational quality, the college appointed a task force on academic excellence, independently of COEP requirements. The job of the task force is much broader than merely responding to such requirements; the task force reviews every aspect of the college that has any impact on teaching and learning and develops recommendations for improving teaching and learning and their outcomes. The task force also develops general guidelines for the assessment of learning in majors and in general education and reviews the results of the learning assessment obtained through the GIS assessment and those in the majors and in general education. An existing task force on general education is developing procedures to assess general education at the program level. A committee on students' personal development and one on community impact have been created to respond specifically to COEP areas where not much assessment has been done at the college.

The executive director of research and planning at the college has been appointed as the COEP liaison. This assignment gives him a dual role—to coordinate the college's activities in responding to COEP, and to provide consultation and support for these activities. Such an undertaking has a major impact on ORP. The impact of the state-mandated programs on ORP is illustrated by the change in focus resulting from COEP requirements—specifically, from support of administrative and management issues to support of the instructional processes of the college. As part of basic-skills assessment and the Cyclical Program Review Process, ORP has worked closely with instructional departments in the college to meet their data needs, but this effort has not entailed much involvement with the instructional process. With the central focus of COEP on assessment of learning outcomes, however, ORP will have to refocus its energies on working closely with chairs and faculty in the instructional departments, in order to develop information on the assessment and improvement of teaching and learning and their outcomes. A researcher with a strong background in educational research has already been hired to work in this area. It has also been decided to publish a journal on a regular basis, in order to provide a forum for sharing information on ideas, procedures, and measures that work toward improving teaching and learning.

The preceding example is a good illustration of how state mandates influence priorities for institutional research at a college. ORP's priorities are set by the president and top administrators. Traditionally, these priorities have involved planning, managing enrollment, generating information on students and personnel for internal and external use, collecting and supplying demographic and labor-market data for the service area, and assessing programs in distress. The latter priority is in keeping with a general tendency to leave instructional programs alone until there is some adverse news or development, such as decline in enrollments, very low graduation rates, low passing rates on licensing examinations, or low employment rates for program graduates. As a result, except in the case of a program in distress, ORP has been and is likely to be more involved with the instructional departments, largely because of external demands, particularly the state-mandated BSAP and COEP.

Advantages of the Model

1. State mandates put pressure on all institutions to undertake assessments of their programs, following agreed-on concepts and directions. Without this pressure, some institutions would not give systematic assessment a high priority.

2. State mandates are more likely to result in increased allocation of resources for assessment at the state and institutional levels.

3. State mandates necessitate common directions for higher education and result in greater research effectiveness and efficiency through central coordination of statewide research activities and collaboration among institutions in developing common assessment procedures and instruments.

4. Extensive involvement of institutional staff and faculty with statewide committees, and exposure to a variety of methodologies and assessment procedures, are likely to raise the level of awareness and expertise at the institutional level. The danger here is the possibility of encouraging conformity in thinking.

5. An institutional decision to respond to a state mandate for assessment, even in a limited area, is likely to have beneficial effects in other areas. For example, setting up an office to conduct assessment, developing data files, and acquiring the ability to analyze data and design instruments

are likely to enable the institution to conduct assessment in other areas. In addition, given these increased abilities and resources, colleges are more likely to generate the information they need to improve their programs. (Some of the data used for program improvement may not be required by the state.)

6. Public reporting of assessment results on some common measures is likely to put pressure on institutions to improve their results. There is the danger that if caution is not exercised in presenting the information, particularly to the news media, gross misinterpretation and misreporting of results may occur.

Disadvantages of the Model

1. Given the need to develop common statewide measures or indicators, the focus could be on what is easily measured through standardized procedures and instruments. This can be avoided, as COEP is doing in New Jersey, by having colleges identify and develop their own goals, procedures, and instruments and by taking the time and providing the resources to do it right.

2. With the state's focus on a limited number of assessment areas and indicators of success, institutions may redirect their efforts and resources in improving results only to those areas where action is requested by the state. This can be avoided if the state mandate is comprehensive and includes a focus on measuring objectives established by the colleges, rather than an exclusive focus on those selected by the state.

3. In responding to a state mandate, some institutions may adopt a compliance mode, spending minimal effort on assessment and thus avoiding a significant opportunity to positively change their programs. This can be avoided if the state monitors the results carefully and if there are some common measures on which institutional performance can be compared. Faced with such comparisons, it will be hard for institutions not to take the state mandate seriously.

4. State-mandated systems tend to focus on accountability measures aggregated at the institutional level and often fail to disaggregate data at the program level, where data have the most meaning. Such systems are also limited to outcome measures, which can help an institution make overall evaluative judgments but are often insufficient for information needed to improve programs.

Conclusion

State leaders have become increasingly interested in higher education and its effectiveness. They view higher education as critical for the state's growth and prosperity, and they want it to have the desired effects. Higher education is no longer considered a personal luxury; it has become a necessity for the survival of individuals and society. Accordingly, state demands for improvement and accountability from educational institutions are likely to increase, rather than diminish.

Accountability measures can put pressure on institutions to improve, but they do not generally tell the institution what to do to improve things. This, however, is the essence of the state-mandated assessment approach: th state monitors results but does not tell an institution how to improve. To improve their effectiveness, institutions must go beyond state requirements and use assessment findings to identify specific areas for improvement.

A focus on outcomes assessment provides institutions an opportunity for self-examination, renewal, reform, and satisfaction. As long as the state concentrates on outcomes, the burden of demonstrating those outcomes will be on the institutions. I would be unreasonable for the state to tell faculty and administrators how to run their colleges, but lack of concern about effectiveness, accountability, outcomes, and program improvement would be equally irrational. The overwhelming majority of state leaders recognize this need for balance between accountability and autonomy. If institutions take the initiative to develop effective outcomes assessment, the need for intrusive state action will diminish.

Finally, let us not forget that neither research nor assessment is our goal; excellence is. Activities that focus on how well students are mastering what they should be learning must be the driving force of our assessment efforts. The stage agency–college-mandated approach to research may foretell how colleges in other states will respond to state concerns for accountability.

Madan Capoor has chaired the New Jersey Basic Skills Council and its assessment committee and is a member of the COEP Student Development Committee.

Edward Morante was a member of the Basic Skills Council, first chair of the New Jersey Basic Skills Council's assessment committee, and director of the Basic Skills Assessment Program.

Community colleges' responses to state mandates for assessment are reviewed, and suggestions for using assessment to strengthen educational programs are presented.

Responding to Mandates for Institutional Effectiveness

Jack Friedlander, Peter R. MacDougall

Past evaluations of institutional performance have focused on such measures as the uses of fiscal resources, expenditures per student, number of volumes in the library, percentage of faculty with advanced degrees, ability levels of students, and job placement and transfer rates of students. In the last six years, there has been a dramatic change in the scope of assessing institutional effectiveness. The focus now is on the extent to which students are achieving the outcomes desired from college attendance.

In a growing number of states, community colleges are required to develop plans to assess students' achievement in such areas as basic skills and remediation, general education, acquisition of knowledge in the major field, personal development, job placement, and transfer to four-year colleges and universities. In addition, colleges are asked to describe follow-up actions for improving their effectiveness in these specified areas. These state mandates—for assessing institutional effectiveness, and for applying assessment results toward improvement in the attainment of desired educational outcomes—will have a major influence on community colleges. Community colleges will need to be prepared to respond. To answer the seemingly basic questions of how students are affected by their college experiences, and of how colleges can use this information for improvements, will require greater levels of institutional support and expertise in institutional research. The purpose of this chapter is to review recent growth in the institutional assessment movement, identify the information on student outcomes that colleges are being asked to produce, describe institutional approaches for responding to state mandates for institutional assessment, and propose recommendations for how community colleges can organize their institutional research efforts to satisfy the mandates for accountability and to improve the effectiveness of their programs and services.

Growth of the Assessment Movement

The growth during the past six years in states that have implemented or plan to implement mandates to assess student outcomes indicates that the movement for institutional assessment is not a fad and will continue (Ewell, 1989a, 1989b). To illustrate, a 1987 study by the National Governors' Association showed that twenty-two states were developing comprehensive assessments of undergraduate learning, and nine states provided institutions with financial incentives to improve undergraduate education; a year later, the National Governors' Association found that only fourteen states had not implemented and were not considering implementing any form of outcomes assessment (Bragg, 1989).

Calls for institutional effectiveness have also come from regional accrediting agencies. Each accrediting agency must determine whether an institution or a program documents the educational achievements of its students verifiably and consistently and systematically applies the information obtained through assessment to foster enhanced achievement (Banta, 1989). These criteria must be considered by all regional accrediting agencies and thus may apply to all accredited community colleges.

In 1985, the Southern Regional Education Board recommended the adoption of statewide course-placement standards, statewide basic-skills testing, and remediation programs for all its members. It also recommended that its members implement statewide exams that end-of-year sophomores must pass to enter the junior year. A number of states (such as Arkansas, Florida, Georgia, New Jersey, Tennessee, and Texas) have implemented statewide basic-skills assessments for all incoming students, while the "rising junior" test has been implemented in Florida and Georgia (Bragg, 1989).

Since 1972, the U.S. Department of Education's Fund for the Improvement of Postsecondary Education (FIPSE) has allocated a substantial portion of its grants to projects on the assessment of student outcomes. The goal of these FIPSE-supported efforts is to have assessment of learning outcomes used as a mechanism for improving colleges and universities nationwide. Cook (1989) has characterized the assessment movement as being perhaps the most significant innovation in postsecondary education in the 1980s. If this movement toward institutional assessment of learning outcomes continues to gain momentum, it will cause colleges and universities to evaluate their programs systematically and continuously. This in turn will heighten the importance of institutional research.

Measures of Student Performance Being Requested by the States

Among the states, there is much variation in the range of outcome measures that community colleges and universities are being asked to assess and in the latitude provided to the institutions for responding to the mandates. In some states, such as Florida and Tennessee, the information to be collected and the procedures for doing so are specified by the state. In other states, such as New Jersey, statewide assessment programs and statewide testing procedures have been established in some outcome areas but not in others. In the majority of states (for example, in Colorado, Kansas, and Virginia), the mandates for assessing institutional effectiveness are in the form of guidelines to categories of the outcomes that must be assessed; measures and procedures for addressing them are left to the discretion of the individual colleges and universities. In this section, we will document the range of performance measures that community colleges are being asked to collect. Knowing the kinds of information used to assess learning outcomes should help community college educators assess the capacity of their institutional research programs to respond effectively to the mandates for evaluation.

In 1983, the Florida State Board of Education established nineteen indicators of progress toward educational excellence for all of its publicly funded postsecondary institutions (see Florida State Board of Education, 1988). The state-mandated measures of institutional performance range from scores on the state-mandated College-Level Academic Skills Test (CLAST) to follow-up studies of college graduates. Other examples of the nineteen indicators are grade point averages in upper-division coursework, job-placement rates of community college graduates, percent of degree-seeking students who are awarded degrees, percent of students who complete preparatory instruction and go on to receive degrees or certificates, results of tests administered to students entering college for the first time, and progress toward student-related goals of the state plan for equal access and equal opportunity.

A system of performance-based funding was established in Tennessee in 1981. Colleges and universities that meet specified performance criteria in each of five categories are eligible to receive additional funds. The amount has increased, from 2 percent of the institution's budget (1981) to 5.45 percent (1988–1992). The performance funding categories are as follows (Tennessee Higher Education Commission, 1987):

1. *Accreditation:* percentage of accreditable programs that are accredited
2. *Major fields and placement:* students' performance on licensing and certification tests; placement of community college graduates in jobs or transfer institutions
3. *General education:* scores of college graduates on the ACT-COMP, a standardized test designed to assess competencies in general education

4. *Alumni satisfaction:* responses, gathered every two years, of the graduating class of two years before to a common survey instrument
5. *Correction measures:* actions taken by the institution to address weaknesses identified in the other standards.

New Jersey has instituted the Basic Skills Assessment Program (BSAP), which contains guidelines specifying the data to be collected and the assessment tests to be used in evaluating the effectiveness of remedial and basic-skills programs (New Jersey Department of Higher Education, 1987a). Under this program, colleges and universities are required to evaluate the effectiveness of their remedial programs, using such measures as the following:

1. Number and percent of remedial students enrolled in the required remedial courses
2. Number and percent of students who successfully complete the final level of remediation in each skill area
3. Results on a test (a different form of the placement test) taken after completion of needed remediation in each skill area
4. Passing rates in subsequent skill-related college-level courses
5. Percent of students achieving grade point averages of 2.0 or higher in college-level courses
6. Percent of students who persist in college.

More recently, New Jersey initiated the College Outcomes Evaluation Program (COEP), a second system for evaluating the extent to which its postsecondary education institutions meet objectives in several categories. The COEP guidelines require all institutions to use a statewide intellectual-skills examination and common measures to assess retention, graduation rates, grade point averages, and units completed. For the remaining components of the COEP, colleges determine their own procedures for assessing their effectiveness in general education; major fields of study; students' satisfaction and personal development; outcomes of faculty research, scholarship, and creative expression; and economic and cultural impact of the institution on the community (New Jersey Department of Higher Education, 1987b).

In Colorado, colleges and universities are responsible for developing statements of institutional goals and objectives for undergraduate education. These are written in such a way that a demonstration of their attainment is possible. Each institution is also required to develop a list of expected learning outcomes, in terms of knowledge, intellectual capacity, skills, and personal development. The institution develops or selects its own measures and procedures for assessing improvement in students' knowledge and skills between entrance and graduation, course-completion and retention rates, and student and alumni satisfaction. Institutions that fail to develop and implement their accountability plans may have their state appropriations reduced by up to 2 percent (Colorado Commission on Higher Education, 1988).

In Virginia, the state has mandated student assessment but allows individual colleges and universities to develop or choose the assessment methods most appropriate to their own diverse characters and missions. In 1987, the State Council for Higher Education in Virginia approved guidelines that required all colleges to develop assessment plans (Miller, 1987). In their plans, institutions are required to identify or describe assessment procedures for general education, assessment procedures for the major, alumni follow-up studies, skills necessary for doing degree-credit work at the institution, evaluation of success in the remediation program, and assessment of the results of the faculty, student, and curricular development programs to address identified problems or deficiencies. As in many other states where mandates for institutional assessment of learning outcomes have been implemented, in Virginia the colleges are expected to show how the information collected benefits students, faculty, and the curriculum. Therefore, in addition to collecting and analyzing data on the various performance indicators, community colleges need to assess how this information has been used to improve college programs.

Responses to State Mandates

Ewell (1989a) notes that responses to state mandates for institutional assessment vary significantly. They range from a compliance mentality (satisfying only minimal reporting requirements) to a more proactive approach (structuring assessment to be used for evaluation and improvement of undergraduate education). According to Ewell (1989a, p. 2), faculty in an institution with a compliance mentality "regard assessment as a bureaucratic reporting requirement—unrelated to real issues of teaching and learning—that can, with some relief, be turned over to an assessment office or an office of institutional research." Other characteristics of the compliance mentality include (1) the decision by faculty to select an existing standardized examination as the primary means of assessing learning outcomes because it is easy to administer and appears to meet state requirements, rather than because it has some relevance to the curriculum; (2) the tendency to regard the assessment process as having been completed when data are collected and forwarded to the state, rather than when the information is incorporated into the institution's processes for instructional improvement; and (3) the attitude that assessment of student outcomes is the first step in a "numbers-oriented statewide accountability plan that [will] ultimately result in common testing, common teaching, and common consequences for those not up to standard" (Ewell, 1989a, p. 2-4).

A growing number of institutions, although still in the minority, are responding to state mandates for measuring achievement by integrating assessment procedures into classrooms, curricula, support services, and decision-making practices (Ewell, 1989a; Hutchings, 1989). As described in Chapter Eight, for example, Middlesex Community College has responded to state requirements by incorporating them into the program-review process. Miami–Dade Community College, as described in Chapter Two, has centralized its institutional research program, linking its response to state mandates with its own efforts to improve students' performance. At the state level, Virginia also has demonstrated the intention to use assessment for the purpose of improving institutions: "The commonwealth has supported institutional autonomy in developing student assessment plans for another reason. Such autonomy makes it possible to go beyond using assessment for the purpose of accountability to an even more important one, the improvement of teaching and learning" (Miller, 1987, p. 37).

Guidelines for Implementing an Effective Assessment Program

The following guidelines are offered to help community colleges establish programs and procedures for measuring students' achievement. The guidelines are based on a review of the literature and on experiences of colleges in states where mandates for assessing outcomes have been implemented.

1. College leaders should be actively involved in shaping the development of statewide approaches to accountability. Leaders' involvement should increase the likelihood that the policies developed for accountability will be flexible enough to meet the state's needs and simultaneously enable diverse institutions to improve teaching and learning. State legislatures appear receptive to such approaches, and the time may be propitious to exert this kind of leadership (Ewell, 1989a).

2. College leaders must be committed to using assessment as a primary means of improving students' learning and development. They must set the tone for regarding assessment as a positive activity that will be integrated into existing operational and decision-making processes. Active involvement of the president and vice-presidents is critical.

3. Colleges should tailor assessment measures to their particular missions, characteristics, and educational objectives.

4. Efforts to assess students' performance should be directly related to teaching and learning. This focus will enable faculty to use assessment results to remedy deficiencies, evaluate and improve the curriculum, and develop better teaching techniques.

5. Faculty, administrators, and staff in student services need to define the goals and objectives of their courses and programs, as well as any learning objectives of the college that include or transcend individual

courses. These objectives should be the basis on which measures of student performance are selected.

6. Faculty and student services staff should be involved in selecting and developing measures to assess students' performance. Their involvement should increase the likelihood of these measures' relevance to educational program objectives and usefulness in improving students' performance.

7. Community colleges should incorporate their data-gathering activities into such existing processes as course examinations, students' evaluation of courses, program review, registration, advisement, and graduation. This approach fosters broad-based involvement of faculty and staff in the assessment process, links data collection to the delivery of instruction and services, and avoids costly and time-consuming testing procedures that are difficult to implement in a community college.

8. Assessment activities should be closely coordinated with any programs for faculty and staff development that are designed to improve students' performance. Classroom research and assessment techniques, as advocated by Cross and Angelo (1988), are one means of connecting programs that assess institutional effectiveness to teaching and learning.

9. Adequate resources must be committed to assessment and to faculty, staff, and curriculum development.

Conclusion

We expect a steady increase in the number of community colleges and universities that will be responding to state requirements for formal, open assessment. Fundamental to our advocacy of institutional assessment is the belief that it will result in improved performance for students: "Assessment should become, over time, an aspect not only of evaluation but of the curriculum itself. Assessment, at its best, can be a learning process for all participants: for the state, which learns which institutions are producing which results; for the institution, which learns how well it is accomplishing the goals it has set for itself; for the individual teacher, who learns where she or he has been effective and where not; and for the student, who develops the capacities for self-reflection and self-evaluation" (Miller, 1987, p. 39). The approach that structures assessment programs to benefit the state, institutions, teachers, and students is the one that we believe should be advanced.

References

Banta, T. W. "Editor's Notes: Weaving Assessment into the Fabric of Higher Education." *Assessment Update*, 1989, *1* (2), 3.

Bragg, A. K. "Beyond the College: State Policy Impact on Student Tracking Systems." In T. H. Bers (ed.), *Using Student Tracking Systems Effectively.* New Directions for Community Colleges, no. 66. San Francisco: Jossey-Bass, 1989.

Colorado Commission on Higher Education. *Policy and General Procedures for the Development of Accountability Programs by State-Supported Institutions of Higher Education as Required by 23-13-101.* Boulder: Colorado Commission on Higher Education, 1988.

Cook, C. E. "FIPSE's Role in Assessment: Past, Present and Future." *Assessment Update,* 1989, *1* (2), 1-3.

Cross, K. P., and Angelo, T. A. *Classroom Assessment Techniques: A Handbook for Faculty.* Ann Arbor, Mich.: National Center for Research to Improve Postsecondary Teaching and Learning, 1988.

Ewell, P. T. "About Halfway: Assessment at the Balance Point." *Assessment Update,* 1989a, *1* (1), 1-2, 4-7.

Ewell, P. T. "From the States." *Assessment Update,* 1989b, *1* (2), 6-7.

Florida State Board of Education. *Florida's Progress Toward Excellence in Education in the State Community College System: A Report to the State Board of Education.* Tallahassee: Florida State Board of Education, 1988.

Hutchings, P. "Linking Assessment and Teaching." *Assessment Update,* 1989, *1* (1), 8-11, 14.

Miller, M. A. *The Virginia Plan for Higher Education: Report on Student Assessment.* Richmond: State Council of Higher Education for Virginia, 1987.

New Jersey Department of Higher Education. *Effectiveness of Remedial Programs in Public Colleges and Universities, Fall 1984–Spring 1986.* Trenton: New Jersey Department of Higher Education, 1987a.

New Jersey Department of Higher Education. *Report from the Advisory Committee to the College Outcomes Evaluation Program.* Trenton: New Jersey Department of Higher Education, 1987b.

Tennessee Higher Education Commission. *Performance Funding Standards for Public Colleges and Universities.* Nashville: Tennessee Department of Higher Education, 1987.

Jack Friedlander is dean of academic affairs at Santa Barbara City College.

Peter R. MacDougall is president of Santa Barbara City College.

INDEX

Accountability, and Miami-Dade central-
ized model, 14. *See also* Assessment
Advantages. *See* Strengths
Agenda, 1; in centralized model, 7-8; in
centralized-decentralized model, 50,
51; in centralized multicampus model,
15-17; in decentralized model, 40-41;
in district-coordinated model, 28-29.
See also Objectives
Allan Hancock Joint Community College
District, 3, 49-57
American River College, 23
Angelo, T. A., 99, 100
Assessment, 93-94, 99; guidelines for,
98-99; movement for, 94; New Jersey
mandate for, 84-85; responses to mandates for, 97-98; of student performance, 95-97. *See also* Mandates

Baker, G. A., III, 21, 22
Banta, T. W., 94, 99
Basic Skills Assessment Program (BSAP),
83, 84, 85, 87, 96
Bragg, A. K., 94, 99

Capoor, M., 4, 83, 92
Changes, 2; and centralized-decentral-
ized model, 54-55; and decentralized
model, 42; and state-local cooperative
model, 79. *See also* Policymaking
Coffey, J. C., 24, 36
Cohen, E., 3, 37, 47
College-Level Academic Skills Test
(CLAST), 15, 95
College Outcomes Evaluation Program
(COEP), 83, 84, 88-90, 91, 96
Colorado Commission on Higher Edu-
cation, 97, 100
Community college transfer study, 68-70
Consortium. *See* Model, voluntary con-
sortium
Consumnes River College, 23
Cook, C. E., 94, 100
Cross, K. P., 99, 100

Defense, Department of, 17
Disadvantages. *See* Weaknesses

District Research Council, 25-28
Doucette, D., 3, 59, 71

Economic impact study, 67-68
Enrollment Management Project, 17-18
Ewell, P. T., 94, 97, 98, 100

Florida State Board of Education, 17, 95,
100
Friedlander, J., 3, 4, 37, 47, 93, 100
Fund for the Improvement of Postsecondary Education (FIPSE), 94

Government: California, 32-33; Florida,
17, 20-21. *See also* Mandates

Hutchings, P., 98, 100

Johnson County Community College
(JCCC), 60, 61, 62, 63, 64, 66, 67, 68,
69, 70
Jones, J. C., 3, 23, 36

Kansas Community College Research Consortium (KCCRC), 59-71

Linthicum, D. S., 75, 82
Los Rios Community College District, 3,
23-36
Losak, J., 2, 13, 22

McConochie, D. D., 3, 73, 82
MacDougall, P. R., 3, 4, 37, 47, 93, 100
Mandates, 1, 4; California assessment,
49-50; Florida testing, 20-21; New
Jersey assessment, 84-85; state assess-
ment, 95-98
Maryland Community College Research
Group (MCCRG), 74-82
Maryland State Board for Community
Colleges, 3, 73-82
Miami-Dade Community College, 13-22,
98
Middlesex Community College, 87, 98
Miller, M. A., 97, 98, 99, 100
Model, centralized, 2; advantages and
disadvantages of, 10-11; implementa-
tion of, 7-10; organizational structure
of, 5-7; procedure in, 10

ORDERING INFORMATION

NEW DIRECTIONS FOR COMMUNITY COLLEGES is a series of paperback books that provides expert assistance to help community colleges meet the challenges of their distinctive and expanding educational mission. Books in the series are published quarterly in Fall, Winter, Spring, and Summer and are available for purchase by subscription as well as by single copy.

SUBSCRIPTIONS for 1990 cost $48.00 for individuals (a savings of 20 percent over single-copy prices) and $64.00 for institutions, agencies, and libraries. Please do not send institutional checks for personal subscriptions. Standing orders are accepted.

SINGLE COPIES cost $15.95 when payment accompanies order. (California, New Jersey, New York, and Washington, D.C., residents please include appropriate sales tax.) Billed orders will be charged postage and handling.

DISCOUNTS FOR QUANTITY ORDERS are available. Please write to the address below for information.

ALL ORDERS must include either the name of an individual or an official purchase order number. Please submit your order as follows:
   Subscriptions: specify series and year subscription is to begin
   Single copies: include individual title code (such as CC1)

MAIL ALL ORDERS TO:
   Jossey-Bass Inc., Publishers
   350 Sansome Street
   San Francisco, California 94104

Other Titles Available in the
New Directions for Community Colleges Series
Arthur M. Cohen, Editor-in-Chief
Florence B. Brawer, Associate Editor

U.S. Postal Service

STATEMENT OF OWNERSHIP, MANAGEMENT AND CIRCULATION
Required by 39 U.S.C. 3685

1A. Title of Publication	1B. PUBLICATION NO.							2. Date of Filing
New Directions for Community Colleges	1	2	1	-	7	1	0	9/18/90

3. Frequency of Issue	3A. No. of Issues Published Annually	3B. Annual Subscription Price
Quarterly	Four (4)	$48 individual $70 institutional

4. Complete Mailing Address of Known Office of Publication (Street, City, County, State and ZIP+4 Code) (Not printers)

350 Sansome Street, San Francisco, CA 94104-1310

5. Complete Mailing Address of the Headquarters of General Business Offices of the Publisher (Not printer)

(above address)

6. Full Names and Complete Mailing Address of Publisher, Editor, and Managing Editor (This item MUST NOT be blank)

Publisher (Name and Complete Mailing Address)

Jossey-Bass Inc., Publishers (above address)

Editor (Name and Complete Mailing Address)

Arthur M. Cohen, ERIC Clearinghouse for Junior Colleges, University of California, Los Angeles, CA 90024

Managing Editor (Name and Complete Mailing Address)

Steven Piersanti, President, Jossey-Bass, Inc., Publishers (above address)

7. Owner (If owned by a corporation, its name and address must be stated and also immediately thereunder the names and addresses of stockholders owning or holding 1 percent or more of total amount of stock. If not owned by a corporation, the names and addresses of the individual owners must be given. If owned by a partnership or other unincorporated firm, its name and address, as well as that of each individual must be given. If the publication is published by a nonprofit organization, its name and address must be stated.) (Item must be completed.)

Full Name	Complete Mailing Address
Maxwell Communications Corp., plc	Headington Hill Hall
	Oxford OX30BW
	U.K.

8. Known Bondholders, Mortgagees, and Other Security Holders Owning or Holding 1 Percent or More of Total Amount of Bonds, Mortgages or Other Securities (If there are none, so state)

Full Name	Complete Mailing Address
same as above	same as above

9. For Completion by Nonprofit Organizations Authorized To Mail at Special Rates (DMM Section 423.12 only)
The purpose, function, and nonprofit status of this organization and the exempt status for Federal income tax purposes (Check one)

(1) ☐ Has Not Changed During Preceding 12 Months	(2) ☐ Has Changed During Preceding 12 Months	(If changed, publisher must submit explanation of change with this statement.)

10. Extent and Nature of Circulation (See instructions on reverse side)	Average No. Copies Each Issue During Preceding 12 Months	Actual No. Copies of Single Issue Published Nearest to Filing Date
A. Total No. Copies (Net Press Run)	2000	2020
B. Paid and/or Requested Circulation 1. Sales through dealers and carriers, street vendors and counter sales	200	43
2. Mail Subscription (Paid and/or requested)	981	784
C. Total Paid and/or Requested Circulation (Sum of 10B1 and 10B2)	1181	827
D. Free Distribution by Mail, Carrier or Other Means Samples, Complimentary, and Other Free Copies	80	178
E. Total Distribution (Sum of C and D)	1261	1005
F. Copies Not Distributed 1. Office use, left over, unaccounted, spoiled after printing	739	1015
2. Return from News Agents	0	0
G. TOTAL (Sum of E, F1 and 2—should equal net press run shown in A)	2000	2020

11. I certify that the statements made by me above are correct and complete	Signature and Title of Editor, Publisher, Business Manager, or Owner *(signature)* Larry Ishii Vice-President

PS Form 3526, Feb. 1989 *(See instructions on reverse)*